VLADIMIR SA

BUILD FIRE

How to Overcome Storms, Setbacks, and Spiritual Attacks

It is easy to recognize someone who walks in heaven's wisdom because their life and words are "pure, peaceable, gentle, open to reason, full of mercy and good fruits, impartial and sincere" (James 3:17). I have found Vlad to be such a person and I'm deeply grateful for his voice in this hour. I was personally refreshed and encouraged as I read *Build Fire*. I believe this book will greatly strengthen and recenter anyone walking through a challenging season. But even if this is not your current situation, trials and persecutions are promised in this life, and I believe this book will prepare and equip you to face whatever storm lies ahead and to endure it while staying aflame for Jesus.

Jeremy Riddle
Worship Leader, Author, and Songwriter

In Philippians 3, the apostle Paul pulled back the core motivation of his life, and from the depths of his heart, he cried, "[T]hat I may know Him and the power of His resurrection and the fellowship of His sufferings." Paul's whole life was about discovering God in every season, no matter how difficult it was. This revelation has been lost in this generation, but I'm so grateful for my friend Vlad Savchuk and his new book, *Build Fire*. What Vlad shares in this book calls us back to Paul's vision of pressing through sufferings and setbacks and continuing to burn for Jesus. God has raised up Vlad for such a time as this, to lead a generation into the fire of a burning heart. This book is a massive gift to all of us.

Corey Russell
Author and International Speaker

We've reached a point in human history in which western culture is rapidly degrading and turning away, not only from the church, but from Jesus Himself. *Build Fire* is a much-needed manual for believers to keep our hearts not only alive, but burning with love and devotion to Jesus throughout the darkest of nights.

Joel Richardson
NYT Bestselling Author and Teacher

Table of Contents

Foreword

This is a serious book for serious readers living in these serious times, written by a man who is serious about the things of God. And while it is full of helpful observations and pithy, bite-size quotes, it is anything but lightweight, providing a way through trouble rather than a way to escape all hardship and difficulty. As Paul and Barnabas said, "We must go through many hardships to enter the kingdom of God," thereby "strengthening the disciples and encouraging them to remain true to the faith" (see Acts 14:22). In short, this is a book for realists wanting real answers to the real challenges of life in this very real world.

What I especially enjoyed about reading this book was getting to know Vlad for himself, since we have not yet met face to face or been in a single service together. Who is the real Vlad Savchuk? Some have warned me to keep my distance from him, assuring me that he is demon-obsessed and not to be trusted. Others speak of him in the highest terms as a real man of God. As I get to know him better, I'll be able to tell you more!

But what I can tell you that is that the author of his book has much to give, not out of theory or speculation, and not simply borrowing from others. Instead, this book comes out of personal life experience, out of years of desiring the things of God, out of years of walking through trials, out of lessons learned the hard way. And when Vlad does quote others, he cites spiritual heavyweights, people who understood the meaning of the cross. What else can help us walk through the valleys and come out victorious? What else can remind us that, above all, God wants to conform us to the image of His Son?

My favorite story comes from early in Vlad's ministry, when after business hours, he and his church colleagues stealthily (and illegally!) snuck into the building they rented for services, careful not to disturb the pastor (who owned the building and lived next door) so they could pray all night. I can relate to this kind of youthful zeal, although I'm thankful that my first pastor was happy to give us a key to our church building when we wanted to pray all night. Still, it is this kind of passion and devotion that can turn into lifelong hunger, the kind of hunger that drives you deeper into God. Quitting or throwing in the towel or compromising is not an option.

I pray that you will find fresh inspiration, encouragement, exhortation, and wisdom as you read this book and that, not only will you learn to build a fire but that you yourself will become a fire. To quote Smith Wigglesworth (1859-1947), "Great faith is the product of great fights. Great testimonies are the outcome of great tests. Great triumphs can only come out of great trials." And this: "Oh, if God has His way, we should be like torches, purifying the very atmosphere wherever we go, moving back the forces of wickedness." May it be so!

Dr. Michael L. Brown
Author, International Speaker,
Host of the *Line of Fire* Broadcast

Introduction

God wants to set you on fire again! When your heart is on fire you are passionate, enthusiastic, have a zeal for the Lord and act on it. I like to compare our hearts to a fireplace. It is meant to warm you. Sadly, the spark of the present flame is absent from the hearts of many believers, leaving only the ashes of the memories of the past. Yesterday's fire becomes today's ashes. Ashes are a sign that the fire is no longer there. They remind us of how good things used to be.

When something is on fire, it is hot and burning. When there's no fire, many people grow cold and turn their hearts into garbage cans where they collect offenses, bitterness, and wrong thoughts. If you remember how you used to love Jesus more than you love Him today, then you have grown lukewarm or may even be backslidden. Remember, your heart was meant to carry the fire, not the ashes. If your heart is not burning for God now, aren't you growing cold? Or have you gotten so cold and passive that you have become the "frozen chosen"? If any of these apply to you, the good news is that you can get on fire again. Jesus commanded the Laodicean church to "be zealous and repent" for being just lukewarm (Revelation 3:19). This was the way to rekindle their fire.

In describing signs of the times and the end of this age, Jesus said, "And because lawlessness will abound, the love of many will grow cold" (Matthew 24:12). This is what we are witnessing all around us in these last days; lawlessness is rising and love and kindness are declining. Dilemmas are everywhere. Truth has become only relative, not absolute. Killing babies in the womb has become a choice and supposedly, a right. Gender has become something a person can decide for themselves instead of discovering their true identity. Suicide and depression among teens have become common and accepted as the new norm. Witchcraft and new age beliefs have become the new trend. The world is going crazy, and that's not a surprise.

Jesus warned us that the love of many would grow cold, which means they will no longer be burning for God. That's a bad kind of growing. It's growing in the wrong direction. It's interesting that growing cold is a process. Growing cold towards God is a serious problem; it doesn't happen overnight.

God said, "I know your works, that you are neither cold nor hot. I wish you were one or the other" (Revelation 3:15). God desires us to be burning and hot. It actually makes perfect sense, since God Himself is a consuming fire and He created us in His image and likeness (1 Kings 18:24 and Genesis 1:26). The first time God appeared to someone in the Scriptures, He took the form of a smoking firepot and a flaming torch (Genesis 15:17). God's Word is also like a fire (Jeremiah 23:29). Jesus is the one who baptizes with fire and the Holy Spirit (Matthew 3:11). The Holy Spirit fell on Jesus' followers as tongues of fire (Acts 2:3). God makes His ministering angels a flame of fire (Hebrews 1:7).

For centuries, fire was used for heating, lighting, cooking, shaping metal, making offerings, getting rid of waste, as a tool in fighting, and other things. Here are a few things that are true of fire:

Fire brings heat. It warms you and everything around you.

Fire brings light. As a Christian, you are called to be a light unto the world. Can you be the light if your fire is missing?

Fire purges. God's fire in you purifies your motives, burning away bad intentions and pride.

Fire spreads. When you catch on fire for Jesus, those around you will be affected. Your flame will warm others and spark a flame inside them as well.

Fire can be extinguished. Paul warns us not to quench the Holy Spirit (1 Thessalonians 5:19). Sadly, some people have become firefighters instead of firestarters.

Fire needs fuel. If you don't put wood on your altar every day, your fire won't burn.

Fire produces smoke. When your life is on fire for God, it produces criticism and attracts persecution and opposition.

Jesus said that being a faithful servant in these last days requires your lamp to be burning: "Let your waist be girded and your lamps burning" (Luke 12:35). We must not run out of oil, and not lose our fire like the five foolish virgins (Matthew 25:1-4). God wants to bring His coals of fire to touch our lips as He did with Isaiah, so that our message will be prophetic to our generation, anointed, and with conviction (Isaiah 6:6-7). Without fiery coals touching our lips, we are nothing but motivational speakers; we are not anointed preachers of the eternal gospel. For a fire to be on our lips, the fire must fall in our personal prayer closets. When Solomon prayed, God's fire came down. When Elijah prayed, God's fire came down (1 Kings 18:38). That fire is sparked in our prayer life and, from there, it spreads to everything else in our life.

We are living in the last days where God wants to set us on fire like Samson set the foxes' tails on fire and sent them into the fields of the Philistine enemies (Judges 15:4-5). Those foxes carried fire and burned everything in their way. Jesus said signs and wonders would follow those who believe (Mark 16:17). Signs, miracles, and the glory of God are in that fire. We must carry it to leave a permanent mark on this generation.

If you've found yourself growing cold and becoming passive in your relationship with God, I pray the Holy Spirit will use this book to pour some holy gasoline on your heart to get you burning again. If you are discouraged, if you've been through a shipwreck or are just burned out, do not give up. The Lord wants to set you on fire again! He loves you so much. I believe He will do just that as you read this book. When the disciples walked and talked with Jesus from Jerusalem to Emmaus, their hearts caught on fire (Luke 24:13-35). The same thing can happen to you. As you read each chapter, I believe the Holy Spirit will kindle a stronger love and devotion for Him. Allow Him to restore the passion that you lost. Not only that, but He wants to give you practical tools to keep on burning for Him and not burn out. When the two disciples got their fire back, they returned to Jerusalem. That happens when you get your fire back; you go back to doing the things you used to do when you had your first love (Revelation 2:4-5).

This book will teach you how to live a life on fire for God; how to soar as an eagle while facing storms and shipwrecks; how to stay on fire in spite of snake bites; and how to not grow cold in the face of difficulties and growing lawlessness. You will explore Paul's troubling journey to Rome, where he endured mistreatment, hardship, and setbacks. You will learn how other men of God who went before us handled calamities, persecution, hardships, and viper bites. They stayed faithful, and so can you! They rose up from their storms, and so can you! They experienced God on a deeper level, and so can you! Remember, we have a whole cloud of witnesses who have finished their race, cheering us on and sharing their testimonies with us.

Therefore we also, since we are surrounded by so great a cloud of witnesses, let us lay aside every weight, and the sin which so easily ensnares us, and let us run with endurance the race that is set before us, looking unto Jesus, the author and finisher of our faith, who for the joy that was set before Him endured the cross, despising the shame, and has sat down at the right hand of the throne of God.

(Hebrews 12:1-2)

CHAPTER I

The Pain of Persecution

Philip Sinyuk was born in 1899 in western Ukraine. In his youth, he came to believe in Christ. He later got married and had six children. In the 1940s, when the Nazis came to occupy his homeland, he was faced with a decision—run and hide in the woods or stay in the village where he lived. While seeking God's direction, a prophecy was given to him during prayer that said wherever he went, God would protect him. So, he decided to stay in the village, and God protected him and his family. The German Nazis didn't care what faith he practiced, as long as he stayed out of their way.

Not long after that, the German army left, and the Soviets came and started harassing Christians for believing in God. They interrupted church meetings, and arrested and fined believers. One day during a church service when Philip was preaching, a Soviet agent came up to him, put a gun to his back, and led him off the stage. Philip was arrested and sentenced to ten years in prison. The charges were preaching the gospel and refusing to join the Communist party. The Soviets viewed Protestants as foreign, western agents and traitors of the regime.

Leaving his wife and six children behind, Philip spent years behind bars. During those years, his wife would send gifts of crackers and flour to the prison. Philip shared those crackers with the other prisoners and put the flour in his bowl of soup, since the only base the soup had was water. Philip was locked up for five years and was released early. However, the hostility toward Christians didn't stop. One day, Philip was walking down the street with his close friend, Gnat. Some Soviet officials in that village were riding in a horse-driven carriage, approached them, and persuasively offered them a ride.

The next thing they knew, the same men in that carriage started to beat Philip and Gnat while the horse was trotting along. Gnat managed to jump out and run into the fields. Philip, while jumping to escape, got his foot stuck in between the wooden planks of the carriage. Instead of stopping the horse to help him get his foot loose, they kept going while his body and head were bouncing on the road. The horse and carriage dragged him for a long time while local field workers watched from a distance. Those men riding in the carriage didn't stop the beating though. They kept giving him lashes as he was helplessly dragged on the road.

After a while, they stopped and dropped him off at a nearby hospital. Philip suffered a concussion and many other injuries to his head and body because of that mistreatment. Due to the seriousness of his injuries, the hospital personnel had to report the case to higher authorities, who opened an investigation. However, the field workers who witnessed the abuse were threatened to be silent. Philip refused to press charges and forgave them, giving them into the hands of God. Five years later, in 1964, Philip died at the age of sixty-five.

Philip was my great-grandfather. His story was passed on to me by his second youngest daughter, Maria, who is my grandmother. She is still alive as I write this book. My grandmother grew up during that difficult time of famine, persecution, and hardship. She has sixteen children (from one husband, by the way) and many grandchildren and great-grandchildren. She is a faithful, on-fire Christian, even in her old age.

Power Comes with Persecution

The apostle Paul was a preacher, missionary, and writer of two–thirds of the books of the New Testament. He was Jewish and had a radical conversion experience. Paul likely became a follower of Jesus sometime in the 30s A.D., which launched him into a ministry that spanned many years, until his death sometime in the 60s A.D. The Lord chose Paul as His vessel to preach to the Gentiles, kings, and the children of Israel. However, this calling also meant that he would suffer much for Jesus' name's sake (Acts 9:10-18).

Paul was used by God in powerful ways, but he also suffered greatly. This great apostle experienced false imprisonments, beatings, stoning, trouble on land and sea, poverty, and much pain. Yet, he bragged about his sufferings as though they were accomplishments (2 Corinthians 11:22-33). To him, suffering and persecution were not signs that something was wrong; they were signs that he was doing something right. They were a fulfillment of Jesus' words to him. It was the price he had to pay to fulfill the purpose of God. For Paul, ministry was a calling, not a career choice. It wasn't about the perks; it was about the price.

Power and persecution usually go together. One can get popularity and never get persecution. One can get prosperity and avoid persecution. But the real power of God that shakes the gates of hell attracts opposition and persecution. Let me say it again: The real, raw power of the Holy Spirit flowing through yielded vessels attracts persecution. Jesus warned His disciples, even as they were going on mission trips under His supervision, that they were sent out "as lambs among wolves" (Luke 10:3). He called His disciples "lambs" in the sense that those who follow Him are called to have a character of humility, while the world is imitating the wolf, whose nature is that of a predator. We are lambs; we are the prey of the world and targets of persecution from religious people, the government, society, and even our own unbelieving family members (Matthew 10:17-22). Yet, that's not how most of us see the Christian life.

Also, people might think being used by God in ministry means that they will have non-profit status, a staff, a salary, and invitations to speak at big conferences. They may write a few books, start a YouTube channel, sell courses, and get verified on Instagram. People pretty much think that being a vessel of God and speaking to kings and to the nations equals popularity and prosperity. Please understand, Jesus told Paul that speaking to kings and nations would come with persecution and pain. In fact, Paul spoke to kings and national leaders as a prisoner bound in chains.

The Promise of Persecution

It's important to highlight that when the Bible talks about persecution, it is referring to hardships endured for Jesus' sake, not for our sin's sake. Some people develop a persecution complex, treating every attack and discomfort as persecution. Some of us are still full of ego, arrogance, laziness, and bad habits, and so we reap the consequences of these things. This is not persecution. We have to be very careful that we don't take Scripture out of context and comfort ourselves in our compromises when, in reality, we should be repenting.

Persecution is when we suffer for righteousness' sake (1 Peter 3:14), for godly living (2 Timothy 3:12), for the kingdom of God (2 Thessalonians 1:5), for being Christian (1 Peter 4:16), and for Christ's sake (Philippians 1:29). Suffering for our stupid decisions is not persecution. I want to point out that Joseph was in jail because he ran from sexual sin, but Samson was in jail because he ran with sexual sin. Both men were in jail, but for very different reasons. Joseph was falsely accused, while Samson deserved all that he had coming to him because he was a womanizer (Genesis 39 and Judges 16).

The word *persecution* in Hebrew originates from the verbs *pursue* and *bear a grudge against*. It is the idea that someone is hunting you down to inflict pain. In other words, it's an ill intent to cause evil treatment. Jesus mentioned three forms of oppression: persecution, reviling, and being spoken evil against.

> *Blessed are you when they revile and persecute you, and say all kinds of evil against you falsely for My sake.*
>
> (Matthew 5:11)

"Persecution" speaks of physical attacks; "reviling" speaks of personal insults; and "all sorts of evil spoken" is falsehood being spread about us.

Physical abuse is the most extreme version of persecution. Remember that Jesus suffered physically through scourging, beating, and being crucified. Throughout history, His disciples have followed in His footsteps. Here are just a few examples from the early church:

- A year after Jesus was crucified, Stephen was stoned to death outside Jerusalem.

- Peter was crucified upside down during the persecution of Nero.

- Andrew died on a cross.

- James, the younger brother of the Savior, was thrown from the pinnacle of the temple and then beaten to death with a club.

- Bartholomew had his skin stripped off while he was alive.

- James, the elder son of Zebedee, was beheaded.

- Thomas, the doubter, was run through his body with a lance.

- Philip was hanged from a pillar.

- Thaddeus was shot to death with arrows.

- Simon died on a cross.

Tradition says that John is the only one who died of extremely old age in Ephesus, yet not without experiencing severe persecution during his lifetime.

These kinds of physical torture, to either punish a person for their faith or force them to renounce their faith, is still common in some parts of the world today. According to the Open Doors World Watch List, more Christians continue to be detained or killed for their faith and more churches closed each year. Throughout last year, over 365 million (that's one in seven believers around the world) experience high levels of perse-cution and discrimination. It is reported that, on average, more than sixteen believers are killed every day for following Christ.

Verbal and emotional abuse is another form of persecution. To be reviled is to be verbally insulted, slandered, mocked, ostracized, and made an outcast. Along with that is the third form of persecution: having all manner of evil spoken against you falsely—being falsely accused, criticized, and discriminated against. Verbal assaults and false accusations are not new to believers. And Jesus experienced all that, too. Religious leaders called Jesus a glutton, a drunk, and one with a demon (Matthew 11:19, Matt. 12:24). He was falsely accused and verbally assaulted. And just like Jesus, His followers often experience the same treatment.

Learn to Endure Persecution, not Just Enjoy Life

There is an abundance of teaching today about how to enjoy life. There is a shortage of teaching about how to endure persecution, reviling, and being spoken evil of falsely. Scripture says of Moses:

> *Choosing rather to suffer affliction with the people*
> *of God than to enjoy the passing pleasures of sin.*
> (Hebrews 11:25)

Moses traded pleasure for pain, success for suffering, and the palace for persecution. He knew that the pleasures of Egypt were a spiritual prison, but persecution with God's people was true freedom. He chose suffering, not because he struggled with a martyr complex, but because that's what was required at that time to identify with God's people. Learning to enjoy life is great, but learning to endure suffering is essential.

The apostle Paul prepared young Timothy not just for success but also for suffering:

You therefore must endure hardship as a good soldier of Jesus Christ.

(2 Timothy 2:3)

We are soldiers in God's army. Military service places restrictions on personal liberties, and so does Christian ministry. Those in the military go through boot camp and crazy amounts of training, and they do endure suffering. Soldiers must develop strong discipline in the midst of it. That discipline is vital to be effective in war. The Christian life is no different. As a good soldier of Jesus Christ, you don't avoid suffering; you learn to endure it. Spiritual warfare doesn't protect you from persecution; it gives you a better handle on it.

There is a story about John Wesley, a leader of revivals in the eighteenth century. One time, he got upset that it had been three days since he'd suffered persecution. No one had thrown a brick or an egg at him for three days. He was so distraught that he stopped his horse and started to pray for God to examine his heart to see if there was any sin or backsliding in him. He went to ask the Lord to show him where his fault was. Right around that time, someone from the other side of the road saw John Wesley and threw a brick at him but missed. John Wesley finished his prayer and—with great joy—got back onto his horse, thanking God that he was still on track with His purpose. What a perspective! Most of us doubt God's presence in the middle of persecution; John Wesley was assured of it.

In the Gospels, Jesus warns us about the sun of tribulation that exposes the weakness in the soil. This persecution scorches the seeds that are planted in the stony ground.

But he who received the seed on stony places, this is he who hears the word and immediately receives it

with joy; yet he has no root in himself, but endures
only for a while. For when tribulation or persecution
arises because of the word, immediately he stumbles.

(Matthew 13:20-21)

Believers who don't mature into disciples of Christ don't know how to endure. They know how to enjoy salvation, but not how to persevere and endure suffering. It takes spiritual growth, maturity, and the right teaching of God's Word to break the stony ground inside us. Tribulation exposes what's already there—no deep roots, and thus, no ability to endure, persevere, or hang in there! We can conclude that persecution is scorching that either *defines* us or *refines* us.

From Persecuting to Being Persecuted

Paul spent his early life persecuting Christians and when he became a Christian, he himself was persecuted. It seems like there is no middle ground; you're either the one persecuting or the one being persecuted. Have you ever thought about this? What if many Christians are not persecuted today because they are the ones doing the persecuting? They believe they are God's anointed and appointed spiritual watchdogs to uproot heresy and falsehood from Christianity. Their criticism (persecution) is the work they think God called them to do.

Yes, the time is coming that whoever kills you will
think that he offers God service.

(John 16:2)

Personally, I get concerned when I don't get criticized. I would rather be persecuted than persecute others. If I am criticized for what God is doing through me, that means I am doing something for His kingdom. If all I am doing is criticizing others, that means I am not doing much—I have too much idle time on my hands. It means I keep looking at what everyone else is doing and have enough time and energy to attack it. I am not saying that we don't need to examine, judge, and evaluate things. But when we don't win souls, make disciples, cast out demons, heal the sick, and build up a local church—but we attack others who are doing those things—something is wrong with our theology. I'm afraid that many have become like Saul, persecuting the church and the move of God, thinking they are doing God a service. Are you persecuting and criticizing, or being persecuted and criticized yourself?

It is time to develop thick skin to handle persecution in the form of criticism. We might not be worthy yet to suffer physical abuse for Christ, but we need to develop the virtues of long-suffering and self-control. Unfair criticism provides the perfect environment for developing those spiritual qualities. The idea that *If I do everything right, everyone will like me* is a myth. Jesus' relationship with the Father and His teaching offended the Pharisees; and yes, you will offend religious people as well as others around you if you are anything like Jesus. There is no way around that. If your goal is to be liked by everyone, then following Jesus will be difficult for you. Sell ice cream instead.

In the early days of our church, we got a lot of criticism for our deliverance ministry (we still do a lot of that now). People commented and said anything and everything you can think of. Most of it came from Christian churches in the area. How tempting it was to preach a sermon to defend ourselves and to react to those critics. However, the Lord led me to the story of King David in 2 Samuel 16. When Shimei came out, cursing continuously and throwing stones at David, David didn't throw them back. The only stone David threw was at Goliath. I also choose to save my stones for Goliath's head, not to hit my critics. God called me to destroy the works of darkness, not the works of critics.

Unfair criticism stings like a mosquito bite, and if I keep scratching that itch, it itches more. Criticism is a trap to lure us away from our purpose into aimless arguments and fights, which produce no fruit whatsoever. It's better to keep on working than to defend our name. When Nehemiah was attacked with slander, criticism, and even threats, he kept on building the wall. He didn't let critics rent space in his mind by giving them much attention. One of my favorite quotes from Nehemiah is:

I am doing a great work, so that I cannot come down. Why should the work cease while I leave it and go down to you?

(Nehemiah 6:3)

By the way, getting defensive all the time is a sign of immaturity and pride. Don't become big in your own eyes and begin to think that you are something. In reality, we are just servants of God, and servants sometimes get mistreated—that's a part of being a servant. Why do we pray for God to make us His bondservant but complain when we get treated as one? We desire to be a bridge to a dying world, but we whine when people walk all over us.

When we are criticized, we must learn to focus on God and seek what He wants us to do, instead of reacting in the flesh. Responding to God takes thought, prayer, reflection, and examination. Stay humble; a humble spirit is required for anyone who wants to grow in God and learn from their critics. Reacting is being impatient, hurt, offended, and retaliating in the name of God. When Jesus was on the cross, his critics made fun of Him and told Him to come down. Remember, He didn't react to them. He didn't yield to their mocking demands. He was living in response to the Father's will, not the people's demands. My personal rule is to pause and ponder before I try to prove and defend myself. And if the criticism is true, I want to learn from it and grow. If it is false, I rejoice and bless.

CHAPTER 2

Saints in the Storm

Horatio G. Spafford was a successful lawyer in Chicago. He was married to a woman named Anna, and they had five children together. He was a big supporter of D.L. Moody, a very well-known evangelist of that day. Despite his success, Horatio was not a stranger to suffering and tragedy. Around 1870, his only son died of scarlet fever at the age of four. The following year, his real estate property suffered extensive damage from a great fire.

Horatio planned a vacation to Europe with his family to get some rest. He booked their trip on the ship SS Ville du Havre. He also committed to help D.L. Moody with his evangelistic crusades. In a sudden change of plans, he sent his family ahead while he stayed back home to resolve some pressing issues. On November 22, 1873, while crossing the Atlantic Ocean, the ship was involved in a collision with another sea vessel—the Loch Earn—and the SS Ville du Havre sank within twelve minutes claiming 226 lives. Spafford's four daughters died. His wife Anna survived and sent him the now-famous telegram, "Saved alone. What shall I do?"

After getting that desperate message from his wife, Horatio set sail for England. The captain of the ship on which he was traveling knew that Horatio had lost his four daughters on the ship that sank. He invited Horatio to the bridge to show him the exact spot where the shipwreck had happened a few weeks prior. As he learned more about the tragic loss of his girls, he rushed into a room and wrote a poem. One of his friends, Philip Bliss, was a vocalist and a songwriter. Philip was so moved by the poem written from such a deeply broken heart that he composed a melody for it and called it, "It is Well with My Soul." Let me recite it:

When peace, like a river, attendeth my way,
When sorrows like sea billows roll;
Whatever my lot, Thou hast taught me to say,
It is well, it is well with my soul.

Though Satan should buffet, though trials
should come,
Let this blest assurance control,
That Christ hath regarded my helpless estate,
And hath shed His own blood for my soul.

My sin—oh, the bliss of this glorious thought!—
My sin, not in part but the whole,
Is nailed to the cross, and I bear it no more,
Praise the Lord, praise the Lord, O my soul!

For me, be it Christ, be it Christ hence to live:
If Jordan above me shall roll,

No pang shall be mine, for in death as in life
Thou wilt whisper Thy peace to my soul.

But, Lord, 'tis for Thee, for Thy coming we wait,
The sky, not the grave, is our goal;
Oh, trump of the angel! Oh, voice of the Lord!
Blessed hope, blessed rest of my soul!

And Lord, haste the day when the faith
shall be sight,
The clouds be rolled back as a scroll;
The trump shall resound, and the Lord
shall descend,
Even so, it is well with my soul.

Affliction and suffering happen to everyone, not just Christians. Think about it; when Jesus was on the cross, there were two others suffering there as well. One was repentant, one was a rebel, and in the middle was the Redeemer. Some suffer because of their own sin; some suffer because of lawlessness and sin in the world. Jesus suffered for sinners. Sinners, saints, and the Savior all experienced suffering. Not everyone suffers for the same reason, and not everyone suffers in the same way. The Christian faith doesn't promise a life without storms or crosses or sufferings, but it promises that God will never leave us nor forsake us. We have a Savior who is perfect and holy, and He is right in the middle of it all with us. If we walk through the valley of the shadow of death, He is the One who walks with us and leads us out; therefore, we fear no evil. He is not in a high castle watching what we go through via an observation telescope. He is in the middle of the storm with us.

For we do not have a High Priest who cannot sympathize with our weaknesses, but was in all points tempted as we are, yet without sin.

(Hebrews 4:15)

Accidents, tragedy, loss, and suffering are all part of life on this earth that is ravished by sin and the curse. God does not create our suffering; He redeems us from the cause of suffering and He never abandons us in the midst of it. Let's be very clear: sin brought all sorts of suffering into the world—not God. It took the suffering of Jesus on the cross to bring about our salvation. If it had not been for sin, there would be no suffering; and if it had not been for suffering, there would be no salvation. Jesus' suffering for us opened the door to our salvation. Jesus not only suffered for us, but He was also called a Man of sorrows and one who was acquainted with grief (Isaiah 53:3). Jesus suffered on the cross in our place to satisfy the wrath of God. Not only was He our Lamb who was slain, but He also gave us an example of how to walk through suffering. Not only is He our Master, but He also modeled how we are to live our life. That's why we are called Christians; our life is to reflect Christ, even in suffering. The apostle Paul tells us to be imitators of Christ (1 Corinthians 11:1), and even our Savior says, "…[L]earn from Me" (Matthew 11:29).

Not a Cruise Ship

The apostle Paul—a prisoner for the Gospel—once traveled on a voyage from Caesarea to Rome (Acts 27). It wasn't a modern-day cruise ship experience. Paul wasn't on vacation. He was placed in the custody of a Roman officer named Julius, a man of good character who allowed Paul to go ashore at some ports to visit his friends and receive care. Luke and Aristarchus accompanied Paul on this journey. The ship stopped at a few places, and then the centurion put them on board a cargo ship sailing from Alexandria to Italy carrying wheat. There were 276 people on board, including the crew.

Encountering heavy headwinds, which made travel very slow, they found a harbor in a place called Fair Havens. This was around late September or early October, during the Jewish feast (Day of Atonement). The time of year indicated the winter's dangerous sailing weather was about to begin. Normally, sailors would wait until winter was over before continuing their journey. Paul warned the crew members in charge that traveling at that time would be dangerous to the cargo and the people on board. He spoke not only under the influence of the Holy Spirit but also as a person who had a medallion status in sea travel. One scholar said that, by that time, Paul had already traveled 3,500 miles by sea. That's quite an accumulation of sea miles!

The centurion decided to heed the advice of the sailors and the owner of the ship instead of Paul, the prisoner. The experts knew best, he figured. Plus, who would want to spend the winter on a small island? At first, everything was fine, and it seemed like Paul had overstepped his boundaries; the experts were right. But then, the violent northeastern wind called Euroclydon engulfed them, and the experts got scared. The storm became a raging hurricane blowing in all directions. Imagine going through a hurricane on a cargo ship! What Paul had warned them about was happening. Unable to steer the ship, they let the storm drive her. They tied cables around the hull of the ship to keep it from being broken apart by the violent waves. For many days, they were tossed by the waves and driven by the wind; it seemed they were at the mercy of the storm. They didn't see the sun or the stars; they didn't know where they were. Soon, all hope of surviving the storm was lost.

Unfortunately, they found themselves in a storm that would bring much suffering and loss. Their suffering wasn't persecution but a natural phenomenon of nature. They could have avoided it if the captain had heeded the wisdom and recommendation from Paul. Now 276 people were facing death, not as punishment from the government for their crimes or convictions of faith, but what some people call the common calamities of life. Storms come to everyone; sometimes we can avoid them, and other times we can't. No matter what storms we face, God is with us in the middle of each one.

Throw Jonah Out!

There have been a number of storms and hurricanes here on earth that have claimed the lives of many and devastated much property. In the Bible, we see three notable, but different, storms: the storm that Jonah was in (Jonah 1:4-16); the storm that Jesus was in (Matthew 8:23-27); and the storm that Paul was in (Acts 27:13-44), which is the one I am discussing in this chapter. By the way, when we read about Paul's life, we find out this wasn't the only storm he encountered.

Let's look at how these storms ended: Jonah's storm ended when Jonah was thrown overboard; Jesus' storm ended when He spoke to it and rebuked it; and Paul's storm ran its course and claimed the ship. As you see, not every storm is the same, and not every storm is overcome the same way.

In Jonah's case, God caused the storm to get his attention. If you remember, Jonah ran from God's assignment to him, thus running from God's presence. His disobedience to God put those on the ship with him in danger. In other words, they almost died because of a prophet's disobedience. The storm wasn't to punish the sailors who were on the ship but to awaken the saint,

Jonah. When we are out of God's will, He will use storms in the world to get our attention and redirect us. He will bring us back to His purpose for us. God disciplines His children when they are disobedient by using painful situations to wake us up. In my book, *Break Free*, I wrote:

Discipline is different than punishment:

- Punishment is eternal; discipline is temporary.
- Punishment is for sinners; discipline is for saints.
- Punishment is out of wrath; discipline is out of love.
- Punishment is later; discipline is now.[1]

Please let me emphasize this again: God does not punish us. He already punished Jesus for all of our sins; and now, as a loving Father, He disciplines us in our rebellion to lead us to repentance. That is what happened with Jonah. In his book, *The Problem of Pain*, C.S. Lewis wrote,

"God whispers to us in our pleasures, speaks in our consciences, but shouts in our pains. It is His megaphone to rouse a deaf world."[2]

Obviously, the storm stopped when Jonah was thrown overboard. He became a "sacrifice" that stopped the storm. After Jonah repented, the Lord gave him a second chance—another opportunity to go to Nineveh. Please understand, some of our storms are caused by our own disobedience, and God can use those storms to get our attention. At other times, storms come because we have a "Jonah" in our boat. I think we have all experienced emotional turmoil—being unsettled in our heart due to having that one person in our life who just needed to go. As much as we don't want to remove them, unless we do, we might be prolonging the storm. Throw "Jonah" overboard and the storm will end. Our "Jonah" might not be a person; it may be a habit, an obsession, or a sinful act that we need to remove from our life. It can be a "Jonah" of disobedience to the voice of God, laziness, unforgiveness, an emotional affair, lying, stealing, cutting corners, etc. God can't bless a mess. We have to play our part and throw every "Jonah" out if we want to experience peace in our heart.

Peace, Be Still

Jesus' storm was different than Jonah's storm. No disciples were thrown overboard, thank God. Jesus was in a storm on the way to the country of the Gergesenes. A great tempest arose on the sea while Jesus was asleep in the boat. The disciples were panicking in the storm; Jesus was sleeping in it (Matthew 8:23-25).

Jesus, the Prince of Peace, had so much peace in Him that He could sleep while waves were crashing around Him. In the same manner, God's peace can guard our heart and mind when the storms of life are raging. His peace is supernatural and surpasses all understanding (Philippians 4:7). You will be able to sleep during your storms. Peace is one of Jesus' gifts to us. He said, "My peace I give to you" (John 14:27).

It takes faith and trust to fall asleep in a storm. I can add that it takes great peace to sleep in the storm, and it takes great faith to speak to the storm. The disciples panicked and woke Jesus up, which was good. Jesus was at peace and rebuked the storm. Let me sum this up: Great faith speaks *to* the storm; little faith speaks *about* the storm. Great faith tells the problem how big God is; small faith tells God how big the problem is. Whatever amount of faith you have, take courage. Wake the Lord up with your cry or silence the storm with your faith.

I believe that the storm they encountered on the way to the Gergesenes was caused by the enemy because when Jesus rebuked the wind, it stopped. Jesus was on His way to deliver two demon-possessed men, and the enemy was most likely trying to hinder His arrival. Satan causes storms to hinder our calling. We must find courage to awaken our prayer life, find peace at the feet of Jesus, and speak God's Word to our soul and circumstances.

Yes, you can speak to your soul. Let me explain. Your soul is very important, and you should not ignore its needs. However, your soul should not be in charge of your spirit. We ought to live by our spirit that is in Christ; therefore, we can speak to our soul. David commanded his soul, "Bless the LORD, O my soul" (Psalm 103:1). Again, in another psalm, he spoke directly to his soul:

> *Why are you cast down, O my soul? And why are you disquieted within me? Hope in God, for I shall yet praise Him.*
>
> (Psalm 42:5)

When you feel distressed, find the peace in your spirit that surpasses understanding so you can speak to the storm in your soul. As Christians, when we are filled with God's Word and with faith, we can speak to our mountains. We can speak to dry bones. We can speak and rebuke the devil who is breathing down our neck, and we can speak to our storms. We have this authority in Jesus.

Let me repeat: When the storm is caused by disobedience or sin, we need to throw "Jonah" out (repent and make a change).

When the storm is caused by the enemy, we need to wake the Lord, get in His presence, and speak to the storm.

Surviving the Storm

Paul's storm was also different from Jonah's because it wasn't caused by his sin or by spiritual forces. His storm could have been avoided. How did Paul get through it? We don't see Paul speaking to this storm. The crew threw the cargo grain overboard, but it didn't do anything to stop the storm or help the ship.

The ship that Paul was on was most likely a freighter taking grain from Egypt to Italy. Well, the ship never made it to its destination. Instead, it struck a sandbar and broke up. However, God gave a promise to Paul:

> There will be no loss of life among you, but only of the ship.
>
> (Acts 27:22)

God promised to preserve the souls of the men on the ship, but not the ship itself.

Paul survived the storm by hanging onto broken pieces of the ship. He had to swim to shore. It didn't look supernatural; it was survival. Yet God was with Paul. Not everything that God is involved in will result in a miracle. Sometimes we will have to learn to swim. Get through a hard time, day by day. Hold on to small pieces of hope. Learn to thank God for His provision in giving us our daily bread—not our daily cheesecake. God's provision is not only in abundance, but also in providing for our necessities—just like Paul. Where he used to sail, he now had to swim—that was the only way to make it through the storm.

If going through persecution for our faith teaches us how to suffer for Jesus, going through life's storms with faith teaches us to survive, endure, and increase our faith. The storm ran its course; there was no supernatural intervention that stopped the storm or preserved the ship. Yet it didn't make Paul less of a man of faith. Sometimes it takes the same amount of faith to swim in the storm as it does to silence it. It takes greater faith to survive a storm than to thrive in life without a storm. Not everyone who is swimming has lost their faith. Not everyone who is struggling has no holiness. Not everyone who is surviving is doing something wrong. Faith is not just something that gives you a supernatural miracle; it also gives you the strength to endure.

CHAPTER 3

Shipwrecked Faith

Viktor E. Frankl was a Jewish man who was born in Vienna, Austria, in 1905. He received his medical degree in 1930 and specialized in neurology and psychiatry. In 1938, Dr. Frankl was arrested by the Gestapo and imprisoned in a concentration camp. He spent the next three years in various camps, including Auschwitz, where he experienced terrible suffering. I visited the Auschwitz concentration camp memorial in Poland while on a ministry trip, and it was a sobering experience. Many years have passed from those events in history, but I still felt death in that place.

Frankl, along with other prisoners, went through immense physical abuse, including beatings and cruel torture, as well as starvation. He was subjected to constant degradation and dehumanization, and he was often made to feel worthless and hopeless. He was required to work long hours in harsh conditions, often with inadequate food and clothing. Many prisoners were killed or executed by the guards and even by other prisoners.

Frankl lost his entire family while in the camps. After WWII, Frankl became one of the most well-known Holocaust survivors, having endured immense suffering and trauma. Amazingly, he resumed his practice as a doctor and went on to write many books. In his book, *Man's Search for Meaning*, Frankl wrote,

> "Forces beyond your control can take away everything you possess except one thing, your freedom to choose how you will respond to the situation."[3]

What happens *in* us is more important than what happens *to* us. Oftentimes, we can't control what happens to us, but we are responsible for what happens inside us. The Holy Spirit takes great interest in working with our attitudes, actions, and reactions during our storms. While we desire to know why something is happening to us, the Holy Spirit desires to produce His fruit of patience in us. That fruit will feed others, mark us as disciples of Jesus, and give glory to God.

Without the Holy Spirit's help, it's terrible to go through a storm. Instead of bearing the fruit of the Spirit, we start bearing grudges. Instead of becoming better, we become bitter. Suffering is like a knife; we either grab it by the blade or take it by the handle. If we grab a knife by its blade, we will cut ourselves and bleed. If we take the same knife by its handle, it becomes a tool, and we can cut bread with it. The help of the Holy Spirit is necessary to turn our storms into our sanctification by training us to respond in "love, joy, peace, longsuffering, kindness, goodness, faithfulness, gentleness, and self-control" (Galatians 5:22-23).

Don't Let Storms Destroy Your Faith

Storms can destroy your ship, but don't let them destroy your faith. The ship can represent your job, business, or even ministry—something that carries you from point A to point B or provides for you. Ships can get broken by the winds of change, leaving you without any support. The enemy is not after your ship; he wants to wreck your faith. The greatest loss is when your faith gets wrecked by the storms of life.

Paul lost the ship in the storm, but he didn't lose his faith. There are people today who "deconvert" from Christianity because they've been hurt by the church. Some deconstruct (the process of leaving Christianity) their faith because God didn't answer their prayers the way they expected. Many stumble and ask, "Why did God allow this to happen to me?" or "If God is so good and loving, why is there so much pain and suffering on the earth?" These are genuine questions, especially when you're going through a storm that destroyed your ship. But behind all of it is the enemy who is secretly working to destroy your fruit and your faith.

Think about it: If God didn't heal your mother and she died and went to heaven, she is in a better place. Don't lose your faith because you lost your loved one. If you lost your job, it might hurt for a moment, but what if God has a better job for you or sees you owning several businesses? Remember, all the trouble you experience with money and your career will end when your time on earth expires. Eternity is very, very long, and it will not matter in heaven if you worked at Macy's or McDonald's to make ends meet. Keep trusting God.

Your faith can sustain you and take you far, so do not lose your faith over losing your job. Even betrayals and heartbreaks in relationships—as painful as they are—shouldn't cause you to have a break in your faith. Ten years from now, you might not even remember the names of those people who hurt you so deeply that you were tempted to lose your faith. Life happens, and some storms are unavoidable. I want to encourage you to not give up or lose your faith when you lose your ship. Don't let the enemy cause you to curse God and die because things got hard (Job 2:9-10).

Paul had been through three shipwrecks, yet his faith was not shipwrecked (2 Corinthians 11:25). He even warned us about those who do lose their faith:

> *Having faith and a good conscience, which some having rejected, concerning the faith have suffered shipwreck.*
>
> (1 Timothy 1:19)

Don't be one of those people who allow circumstances in the natural to break their spirit. May your faith stay strong when you lose your ship in the storm. All the things we lose here on earth will be restored to us in heaven, but if we lose our faith, we are toast!

"Even if" Faith

The "faith chapter" in the Bible is Hebrews 11, which starts by mentioning faith at the dawn of history—the faith of Abraham, the faith of the patriarchs, and the faith of Moses—and then lists how people in many generations overcame by their faith. I love the honesty of the Bible because it doesn't stop with visible victories. It goes on to list that:

Others were tortured, not accepting deliverance, that they might obtain a better resurrection. Still others had trial of mockings and scourgings, yes, and of chains and imprisonment. They were stoned, they were sawn in two, were tempted, were slain with the sword. They wandered about in sheepskins and goatskins, being destitute, afflicted, tormented—of whom the world was not worthy. They wandered in deserts and mountains, in dens and caves of the earth.

(Hebrews 11:35-38)

Why would such an optimistic, faith-building chapter end on such a gloomy, negative note? Some received great things in faith, but others did not, even though they had faith.

We can conclude that faith is not always a bridge over troubled waters, but sometimes it's a path right through them. The same faith that enables some to escape trouble enables others to endure it. The same faith that delivers some from death enables others to die victoriously. The same faith that empowers one to stop the storm enables another to survive it.

I call this "even if" faith. The book of Daniel tells us about three young Hebrew men who had this type of faith during their captivity in Babylon.

If that is the case, our God whom we serve is able to deliver us from the burning fiery furnace, and He will deliver us from your hand, O king. But if not, let it be known to you, O king, that we do not serve your gods, nor will we worship the gold image which you have set up.

(Daniel 3:17-18)

These Hebrew guys didn't doubt God's ability to supernaturally keep them from going through the fire. But even if He didn't, their faith in Him wouldn't stop them from trusting Him through the flames.

Fear asks, "What if God doesn't come through?" Faith says, "Even if I have to go through the fire, I will trust Him." God didn't stop the fire in the furnace, but He kept the fire from killing them. His presence was with them in the midst of it. The three Hebrew boys came out of that fire without even the smell of smoke. You can see that it takes faith to go through fire and come out without a smell. It takes faith to go through the valley and not get stuck there and develop bitterness. It takes faith to go through the flood and not drown in doubt, but come out on the other side, washed. It takes faith to not quit in the storm, but to swim through it.

The same thing happened to Paul. His faith didn't prevent the storm and it didn't supernaturally stop the storm. His faith helped him to endure it, not avoid it. God didn't stop the storm, but He didn't let it kill Paul. God was with Paul in the middle of that storm, just as He was with the Hebrew boys in the furnace. As He was with the disciples in the boat during the storm, so He was with Paul.

The presence of the storm doesn't mean the absence of God. Jesus said, "I am with you always, even to the end of the age" (Matthew 28:20). Jesus doesn't jump ship when the storm comes. He never leaves us, but that doesn't mean we won't need to learn to swim!

Faith is *Refined* by Trials, not *Defined* by Trials

What was Paul's secret to enduring suffering? How did he withstand storms? Well, he answered that question in one of his letters:

> *For this reason I also suffer these things; nevertheless I am not ashamed, for I know whom I have believed and am persuaded that He is able to keep what I have committed to Him until that Day.*
>
> (2 Timothy 1:12)

Paul didn't become ashamed, offended, or disappointed in God because of the storm or the suffering he endured. He firmly knew in whom he believed. From a young age, Paul knew the Scriptures thoroughly; Paul was a theologian. When he became an apostle, he wrote letters to churches, which help us know what to believe. But I want you to note that his faith wasn't in doctrines, traditions, or information—it was in a Person. That's what gave him an anchor in the storm. Faith is more than a subject you study; it's knowing Jesus and putting your trust in Him. Jesus invites people to believe in *Him*, not just believe in *something*.

Storms won't destroy true faith; they can only purify it. If you live surrendered to God and in communion with Him, you are like a tree planted by the rivers of water (Psalm 1). Storms will reveal how deep your roots are. Genuine faith in God can't be destroyed by trials. When people claim they lost their faith because of a very difficult time, I wonder if they had genuine faith in God in the first place. I don't doubt they had faith, but many have faith in their faith, or faith in themselves, or their faith is based on their emotions rather than God's Word. Peter wrote:

In this you greatly rejoice, though now for a little while, if need be, you have been grieved by various trials, that the genuineness of your faith, being much more precious than gold that perishes, though it is tested by fire, may be found to praise, honor, and glory at the revelation of Jesus Christ.

(1 Peter 1:6-7)

Gold doesn't grow in size when it goes through fire; it grows in value because it becomes purified. Fire can't destroy gold; fire destroys the impurities in gold.

Faith is like a tea bag; you don't really know how genuine it is until it goes into hot water. Trials reveal your faith, but they also refine your faith. Don't let your storm *define* you when it's meant to *refine* you. You are defined by Jesus' love for you, not by what you're going through.

The Fruit of Longsuffering

One of the reasons people lose their faith so quickly in a storm or shipwreck is because of bad theology. We, as ministers, don't teach people enough about how to endure suffering; we only teach them how to be successful. Many paint Jesus as someone who will make all your problems go away—there will be no pain, no suffering, and no difficulties. Such theology is not biblical, and it confuses Christians who do get slammed by life's storms.

Those of us who are in churches where miracles happen, and where they are expected, should not think that having God's power in our life means we will avoid storms. Paul was a man of power and faith, yet he had lots of afflictions (2 Corinthians 6:4-10). When we witness the power of the Holy Spirit in healing the sick, driving out demons, and raising the dead—pretty much bringing supernatural solutions onto the scene—we can quickly develop unrealistic expectations that if the Holy Spirit does these power deeds for others, He will stop the storms in our life.

That's like the mocking accusation the critics yelled at Jesus: "If You are the Son of God, come down from the cross" (Matthew 27:40). Similarly, the devil told Jesus in the wilderness, "If You are the Son of God, command this stone to become bread" (Luke 4:3). Don't suppose that you can use the power of the Holy Spirit to keep yourself from difficult situations. Some may think the more power of the Holy Spirit we have, the fewer problems we will encounter, but that's not true!

The Holy Spirit, who does miracles through us, doesn't always prevent us from suffering. The Holy Spirit is not always interested in removing suffering but in improving our ability to suffer successfully. One fruit of the Holy Spirit is longsuffering—not avoiding suffering (Galatians 5:22). Let me say this again: The more of the Holy Spirit's presence we feel doesn't mean the less suffering we will go through. It just means that if we are to go through suffering, the Holy Spirit will help us to endure and bear holy fruit. The Spirit of God will help our actions and reactions during suffering—to honor and reflect Jesus.

That's why the Bible spends little time answering the "why" of suffering and deals more with the "how" of suffering. When you read the book of Job, you see a lot of questions about suffering, yet God didn't answer those questions directly. God allowed Job to experience His glory, which left him speechless. God provides us with an experience of His love in the midst of suffering.

It's not that the "why" doesn't matter to God, but oftentimes, we don't need an explanation—we need a revelation of who He is. We need tangible help in our suffering, not just understanding.

Please realize that God sent us a Savior to die for our sins, and He sent us His Spirit to comfort us in our suffering. When storms come and our personal comforts fail, the Holy Spirit is our Comforter—He is always near to us. He is there to remove the pain and carry us through the storm on His wings of love.

If you are currently going through a difficult time, or if you lost your ship and are in despair, God wants to restore you. He didn't leave Paul drifting in the middle of the sea. He restores the brokenhearted because He is the Man of sorrows who took upon Himself the deepest pain of the human heart (Isaiah 53:1). You don't have to carry it anymore. You will get through your storm purified and strong. Pray with me:

Lord Jesus, thank You that You are always with me, even when I don't feel it. You are my Lord and my Savior. Right now, I give You the pain of what happened to me. I give You the pain of (name it). All of it. I receive Your healing oil in my heart, and I forgive everyone who has sinned against me. I renounce bitterness, doubt, and any unbelief that the devil has sown in my heart during this storm. Restore my heart, my strength, and my life in the aftermath of this storm. I know in whom I believe. You are my Healer, my Comforter, and my Lord, and I trust You with my life. Amen!

CHAPTER 4

Don't Starve in the Storm

Have you ever heard the story about the donkey and the dry well? Once upon a time, a farmer's donkey fell into an empty well that had been dry for a long time. For hours, the animal cried out in distress while the farmer tried to do something to save him. Nothing worked. The farmer eventually gave up and decided the donkey was too old and that getting the animal out of the well wasn't worth it. He decided to bury the donkey alive and called his neighbors to help him shovel dirt into the well. Surprisingly, as they began to do so, the donkey started shaking off the dirt and taking a step upward with each shovelful. In no time, the donkey climbed out of the well, much to the amazement of the farmer and his neighbors.

The moral of this story is that life will knock us down; the enemy will try to bury us with the dirt of our problems, but we can get out of the deepest pits if we don't give up. We shouldn't play by his rules and take on the role of a victim. Self-pity will not solve anything. We can use the dirt thrown at us as a stepping stone to climb higher and move forward. The choice is ours. We can either surrender to God or slander Him.

Choose to shake off apathy, complacency, offenses, self-pity, and condemnation. Stand on God's Word and persevere. Even if life doesn't get easier, you will get stronger.

Don't Lose Your Appetite While in the Storm

When Paul and the crew were going through the storm that almost took their lives, one thing they had to do was eat. To survive the storm, they needed to end the starvation. One of the first things Paul urged the men on the boat to do was to eat.

> *And as day was about to dawn, Paul implored them all to take food, saying, "Today is the fourteenth day you have waited and continued without food, and eaten nothing. Therefore I urge you to take nourishment, for this is for your survival, since not a hair will fall from the head of any of you."*
>
> (Acts 27:33-34)

Paul was pretty much saying, "You can't survive the storm if you're starving yourselves. You've got to eat something if you are to make it through."

Going through a spiritual storm can steal your spiritual appetite for God's Word, leaving you with no desire to read and no motivation to even open the Bible. While it can be normal to feel that at times, staying in that mood is extremely dangerous to your faith and survival. If you are to survive, you must eat. By eating, I am referring to reading God's Word. The Bible is your spiritual food—the food that keeps you alive in a storm.

Sometimes you can speak God's Word to the storm, and the storm will stop. Other times, you must feed yourself with God's Word to be able to swim and come out of the storm. All storms come to an end, but you must not come to an end spiritually by starving yourself.

It's one thing to lose your ship in the storm; it's totally different to lose your appetite for God. Then you will die—not because of the storm, but from starvation. Spiritual starvation has killed more Christians than any storm. Don't let your storm starve you.

I've noticed that one of the most common problems among believers is a lack of desire to read God's Word—the ability to spiritually feed themselves. This can happen when our life takes a drastic turn for the worse. Other times, it's just our carnal nature that doesn't want anything to do with the things of God. A storm does not necessarily cause the loss of appetite; our flesh fights against the desire for God's Word. As spiritual hunger goes away, starvation settles in.

The enemy is after your appetite to cut you off from the source of your strength. If he can't kill you with a storm, he will switch tactics to make you kill yourself through starvation. And if, while starving, you blame God for it, the devil gets a double win. A storm can be used as an excuse to not feed yourself spiritually, but it is nothing but an excuse.

The less you read the Bible, the less you desire to read the Bible. The hunger for God's Word comes from consuming it, not avoiding it. Physically, you get hungry by not eating. Spiritually, you get hungry by eating. To get the desire for God's Word, you must read it. Here is my simple solution to increase your hunger for the Bible: You must feed yourself with it. Even if at times you need to force-feed yourself, so be it.

Determine to read God's Word even when you don't feel like it. Following your feelings only reinforces immaturity. Your feelings are the lowest parts of your nature, so don't make them a foundation. We are called believers, not feelers. We belong to the house of faith, not the house of feelings (Galatians 6:10). God has given us a spirit of faith, not a spirit of feelings (2 Corinthians 4:13). God has given us a measure of faith, though not all receive the gift of faith, and He has called us to live a life of faith (Romans 12:3; Romans 1:17). To some, He has given the gift of faith (1 Corinthians 12:9). Wallowing in our feelings might feel good for the moment, but the price for that is spiritual starvation.

The devil knows that he can't defeat a person unless he disarms that person. Satan didn't defeat Eve until he disarmed her by making her doubt God's Word, which led to her disobeying God. On the contrary, Jesus defeated the devil in the wilderness by disarming him with Scripture. Please understand that when you focus more on your feelings than your faith, the devil will rule your life through your senses. But as you feed yourself with God's Word—even when you don't feel like it—God's peace will rule in your heart. You might be in a storm, but the storm will not be in you, because you are strengthened by the Word of God.

The Bird is After the Book

Jesus revealed a great mystery to His followers in the parable of the sower, the seed, and the soil (Mark 4:2-20). There are four types of soil, and each represents the heart's responsiveness to the Word of God. There is hard ground, stony ground, thorny ground, and good ground. The first type of ground is hard, like concrete. It represents hearts that are hardened by pride, indifference, and sin. Hard ground was along the path;

Don't Starve in the Storm

it's where people walk. Those hearts allow life to leave its mark on them. Circumstances walk all over the soil of hard ground. When the Word falls on this type of soil, the birds steal the seed. This is the only ground where birds get fed at the expense of the ground being deprived of the seed.

One time, as I was reading this parable, I felt the Holy Spirit speak to me. He said, "Don't feed the bird; feed your soul." What does that mean? When we hear God's Word and don't feed our soul, we feed the birds. A bird represents the enemy. It's not that the devil wants to be fed by God's Word; it's that he wants to steal it from you. He gets empowered when you and I are starved. That way, he doesn't have to destroy us; we destroy ourselves by being malnourished.

We are like soil; we can't bear fruit unless we receive a seed. A seed can't produce fruit until it gets into the right soil. Without the right soil, we are fruitless, period. When your heart doesn't receive God's Word, the bird gets the meal. Not only do you lose the opportunity to bear fruit, but your spiritual life gets weaker and the enemy gets stronger. When you starve your spirit, you feed your issues. When you starve your faith, you feed your fears. The bird is fed when you are starved. Feed your spirit; the seeds have been provided for you. Don't give any food to the enemy.

The enemy can't stop God's Word from producing fruit in you, so he will fight to ensure that the Word of God doesn't take root. Please understand, once the Word takes root, there is nothing he can do.

- The Word is powerful and sharp (Hebrews 4:12).
- The Word recreates our life (James 1:18; 1 Peter 1:23).
- The Word removes guilt (Ephesians 5:25; John 15:3).
- The Word activates faith (Romans 10:17).

45

- The Word brings growth (Acts 20:32).
- The Word renews our mind (Psalm 119:105, Psalm 1:2, Romans 12:2).
- The Word elevates our mood (Romans 15:4).
- The Word helps us to not sin (Psalm 119:11).
- The Word sets us free (John 8:31-32).

No devil in hell can stop the Word of God from producing these things in your life. Therefore, the enemy's aim is to stop the Word from taking root. Stealing one's desire for God's Word is one of his most malicious tactics, and sadly, one of his most profitable.

Strengthen Yourself in the Lord

When David returned to Ziklag from a military trip, he found that he and his men had lost their families to the Amalekites. All his mighty men were grieving. They had lost their city to fire and their families to the raid. David was in one of the greatest storms of his life; he was distressed, and on top of that, his warriors spoke of killing him. David's solution was to feed himself.

But David strengthened himself in the LORD his God.
(1 Samuel 30:6)

While others sought someone to blame, David sought the Lord for strength. It's interesting that it doesn't say the Lord strengthened David, but David strengthened *himself* in the Lord. God will not force Himself on you when you are in distress. He will always be there, but you have to make a conscious decision to feed yourself on His presence and on His Word. Don't wait on God to renew you; He is waiting on you to renew yourself by drawing near to Him.

David found his strength in God and then he went to inquire of Him. God spoke to him with clear instructions. I have noticed many times that a discouraged soul can't receive instruction from God. A starved soul can't get any direction. God wants to feed you before He can lead you, but you must be renewed in your strength before you can receive your next steps. It was after Jesus was filled with the Spirit at the river Jordan that the Holy Spirit led Him into the wilderness. We rush into trying to hear God when we are not even near Him. We get so desperate for a solution when what we need first is strength.

How can you strengthen yourself in the Lord? One of the ways is by worshipping God. Look at the lyrics of the song Moses sang after God parted the Red Sea: "The LORD is my strength and song, and He has become my salvation" (Exodus 15:2).

If you want to find strength in God, begin to worship Him. Remember that while you are in prayer you may draw near to God, but when you worship, God draws near to you. He seeks worshippers who will worship Him in spirit and in truth (John 4:23). David worshipped God in the most difficult storms of his life by turning his full attention to the Lord. Do you doubt that it's possible? Read the psalms he composed.

Another way to strengthen yourself in the Lord is by praying in tongues. By the way, David did not have that option; that privilege was given to the people in the New Testament, and it is for us today.

He who speaks in a tongue edifies himself, but he who prophesies edifies the church.

(1 Corinthians 14:4)

The word "edifies" here is the same word for "build" that is used in reference to Jesus building the church and the wise man building his house on the rock (Matthew 16:18; Matthew 7:24). You can build yourself up by speaking in tongues.

Do you feel empty, discouraged, or disappointed? Pray in tongues. Don't starve yourself when going through a storm; instead, take a stand on God's Word and strengthen yourself in the Lord. Even if you are not currently in a storm or wilderness, keep strengthening yourself in the Lord your God by speaking in tongues.

CHAPTER 5

Build a Fire

L et me begin this chapter with the biblical account of Michal, the daughter of King Saul, which is found in 1 and 2 Samuel. Born into a wealthy family, her father was the first king of the nation of Israel. Having your dad as the king must have been incredible. Growing up in the palace had its perks. Michal had an older sister named Merab, who was promised in marriage as part of the reward package for whoever killed the giant, Goliath. The guy who finally slayed the giant and saved the nation was not only brave and gifted, but also good looking. Oddly, her father, King Saul, changed his mind and matched Merab with someone else. Well, that was to Michal's advantage because she liked David a lot. Actually, she loved him. He was the man of her dreams—spiritual, romantic (he could play an instrument and sing), fearless, and great looking. In addition to that, David started climbing the corporate ladder pretty fast. He became super famous and everyone liked him.

Michal's dream came true. Her dad agreed to give her to David in marriage, but first David had to work for it. Since David didn't have a dowry (in the old days, the man had to pay the girl's father a sum of money to marry his daughter), he went on a killing spree to the enemy camp and brought back 200 foreskins. Finally, Michal and David were officially married. However, their happiness didn't last very long. King Saul not only had some serious mental problems and demons, but he became extremely jealous of David's fame and victories, and he wanted to kill David. Michal was torn between honoring her dad and her husband. To save David, Michal helped him escape and put a mannequin in their bed. That bought him some time to run and hide. However, instead of following her husband on his unknown adventures, she stayed in the palace with her crazy dad and comfortable bed.

One thing soon led to another. While her husband, David, was on the run and being chased relentlessly by her father, King Saul decided to make things worse and gave Michal in marriage to a man named Palti. Instead of waiting for David to come back, she was married to someone else. Time passed and her father, King Saul, along with some of her brothers, died in battle. It was a tragic family loss. Next, her older brother claimed the throne but his rule didn't last very long; someone cut his head off. It was another brutal death in the royal family.

When the nation of Israel was about to make David their king, he had one request of them: bring back Michal, his wife, who happened to be married to another man. Some may say that was weird and awkward, but the king's command had to be obeyed. Palti—the second husband of Michal—accompanied her and wept until he was told by Israel's general to go home and get over it.

Hang in there—now we are getting to the good part. Michal went back to David, her first love and her first husband. From the outside, she seemed very lucky. She was a daughter of the king, and now she was the wife of a king. The woman was back in the palace, except now as a wife, not just a daughter. Her husband was not a mentally unstable maniac, but a man of God. But Michal's luck was about to change.

There came a time when David was bringing God's ark of the covenant to Jerusalem, and Michal stayed at home and watched the procession from a window. David was full of joy, leaping and whirling before the Lord, but in her eyes, he was acting more like a fool than a king. She watched all that from a window, and the Bible says she despised him in her heart.

I think it was offense and bitterness that created coldness in her heart toward God. While in exile, David had married other wives and had kids, but there was no indication that he asked Michal's input on those decisions. David returned to become the king and he demanded her back, almost treating her like property. He selfishly tore her away from her loving husband. On top of all that, her father, who had mental issues, died. Her brothers died in battle also—too much drama and trauma. She had the perfect excuse to build an offense toward God. Sadly, in all the storms of her life, Michal didn't feed herself on the promises of God—she didn't strengthen herself in the Lord, and she didn't worship Him—she became a window-watcher instead of a worshipper. Passive instead of passionate. Spectating instead of participating. Caring more about dignity than divinity. How many people today do the same and allow the problems in their life to kill their passion for the Lord?

No wonder the Bible calls her Saul's daughter instead of David's wife. She was both a daughter of Saul and a wife of David. Her dad was crazy in a bad sense, and her husband was crazy in a good sense. She chose to reflect the heart of her father, Saul, who was a chronically insecure, people-pleasing, priest-killing, tormented, and dysfunctional king. You probably noted that she showed some of the same characteristics as Saul. She was more concerned with what people thought than what God thought. Her heart was discontent instead of on fire for God. After her verbal attack on David, who was her husband but also God's anointed, she never had any children. She was the daughter of a king and then the wife of a king, but she never became the mother of a king. She remained childless throughout her entire life. I believe it was because of her passive attitude toward the Lord.

Let's learn from this biblical account. While there is nothing you can do about the past, you don't have to let it steal your future by allowing it to quench your fire for God. Generational curses that you've encountered—you are in line to break them! The dysfunction that has run in your family, and run into you, can end with you. Poverty, sickness, divorce, and mental illness that may have been around you all your life don't have to be your destiny. There is a way to break that. Stop identifying yourself with the habits of your ancestor, "Saul," and begin to take on the nature of your Husband—Jesus. You can't beat your family's demons if you don't embrace the new name and lifestyle of your Husband, King Jesus. By the way, Jesus was a lineal descendent of King David and was called the Son of David; prophetically speaking, He is your Husband.

It's your choice to reflect David in passion or be a window-watcher who is passive toward the things of God. When you put on the garment of praise, you will break the curse of passivity. Yes, window-watching is comfortable, but it's a cancer to your future. It will steal your destiny. Remember, you can't go back and change things, but you can see God move in your future if you let Him rekindle the fire in your heart. The future belongs to those who have a flame. Destiny from God is for those who have devotion. If you lose your fire, you will lose your future. Intimacy produces fruit; if there is no passion, there will be no intimacy. You are anointed by God to birth something. Birth a revival. Birth a ministry. Birth a movement. But you can't birth anything if you are just window-watching, making excuses, or blaming someone else for why you are not burning for God.

Stop being a window-watcher. Let me recall for you three women in the Old Testament who looked through a window: Sisera's mother (Judges 5:28), Saul's daughter, Michal (2 Samuel 6:16), and Jezebel (2 Kings 9:30). All three opposed God's will and suffered accordingly. God called you to be a passionate worshipper, not a window-watcher.

Build a Fire, Not a Ship

Let's go back to our story of Paul and his shipwreck. When he survived the shipwreck and the storm, he landed on an island called Malta. This is a small island, around ninety-six square miles, that lies about fifty miles from Italy and 207 miles north of Libya. The first thing the survivors did on the island wasn't to look for another ship to resume their journey to Rome. Instead, they built a fire. It was cold and raining, and the fire helped them to get warm.

Sometimes when we lose our ship in a storm, we are tempted to try to rebuild it, instead of building an altar. We're in a hurry to rebuild our life. We try to recoup our losses rather than recover our spiritual strength. We love to make excuses for why we can't build a fire. Life can become like a rollercoaster with many twists and turns—a dysfunctional family, wounded hearts, lost jobs, broken relationships, betrayal from those closest to us, hurt from church people, etc. The more we make excuses, the more we settle for passivity. It makes sense to guard our heart from getting hurt again, but hardening it is dangerous. When life's not been fair, we let the fire die. When we're not careful, we can let the drama we've lived through kill our devotion to God.

Paul was on his way to Rome, and the shipwreck was a huge detour. Even though he survived the shipwreck, it put a huge delay in his court case. Still, he didn't waste his time there. He spent his time waiting on the island of Malta—waiting and ministering. After three months, they found another ship and finally made it to Rome (Acts 28:1-11). Sometimes when we survive a storm, we are in a hurry to get back everything we lost. Instead, we can use that time to cultivate a deeper hunger for the things of God without forsaking our duty to rebuild our ship of faith.

Building a fire should be the first priority. Let go of the offense—don't look back to what you've lost; look at what you have left. Even if you only have a spark, that spark must turn into a flame. Fan that flame. Feed that flame. Don't let a storm steal your fire. Don't let a shipwreck make you cold toward God. In due time, you will set sail again.

Build an Altar and Pitch a Tent

Throughout the Old Testament, people built altars for several reasons. Some were to remember God's goodness, to worship Him, or to offer a sacrifice. Every altar was an expression of relationship with God. Abraham, our father of faith, demonstrated this so well. It says of him that everywhere he went, he would build an altar and pitch a tent. Here is just one example:

*Then Abram moved his tent, and went and dwelt by
the terebinth trees of Mamre, which are in Hebron,
and built an altar there to the LORD.*

(Genesis 13:18)

Building speaks of something permanent, but pitching a tent is temporary. Anytime you go camping and set up a tent, it's for a short time. A tent is a temporary residence, not a permanent dwelling place. We build houses but set up tents. That's how normal people live. Abraham wasn't normal. He built altars for God, but he treated his own dwelling as something temporary. Someone may argue that everyone lived in tents in those days. That's true. The author of Hebrews tells us that Abraham dwelled in tents, waiting for the city whose builder is God (Hebrews 11:9-10). Though he was rich in wealth, he had his priorities in order: building an altar and then pitching a tent. The only thing that was permanent in his life was the altar; everything else was temporary. He was building his altar—his fire—his relationship with God. His house, wealth, and riches were simply tents—temporary dwellings. In the New Testament, the apostle Paul also referred to our body as a tent that will be destroyed (2 Corinthians 5:1).

When you're building an altar, you are not attaching yourself too closely to any place, people, or possessions. Some people are addicted to a stage but allergic to an altar. They love positions in church more than prayer. They love titles more than they love Jesus. They love connections more than communion with the Holy Spirit. They love possessions more than the presence of God. They love their own life more than they love the Lord. Jesus warns us that those who love their life will lose it (John 12:25). To gain this life is to lose it (Matthew 10:38). We shouldn't have an affair with the temporary things of this world at the expense of putting God in second place. Life and everything connected to it is as fleeting as the wind (Job 7:7), as temporal as grass (1 Peter 1:24), as lasting as a flower (Job 14:2), as passing as a shadow (Ecclesiastes 6:12), and vanishes as a vapor (James 4:14). Death is as water spilled (2 Samuel 14:14). Life on earth is temporary and it should be treated as such. God is eternal; He should have the supremacy.

One of the reasons many people don't have time for God is because they occupy that time with something else. If the Lord doesn't occupy the place of prominence, things will. The place of priority is never vacant. Someone always takes first place. The throne of our heart never stays empty. We should always examine our hearts to see what we are building and what we are pitching so that we don't end up pitching our altars and building our tents.

When People Leave

When you build a relationship with the Lord, it helps you to navigate constant transitions in life. Your relationship with Him must be first, no matter where you are or who is with you. Those who don't build altars to the Lord will become too dependent on people. The fear of man will start to rule people who lack the fear of God. Let me emphasize again, Abraham built an altar and pitched a tent. So, when his nephew Lot left him, Abraham didn't panic; he lifted his eyes and saw God's promise. Lot, whose name means "veil" or "covering," didn't have an altar in his life.[4] In fact, it seems like Lot didn't pursue God the way Abraham did. He pursued his own ambition. He lifted his eyes when he planned to separate from Abraham and saw the land of Sodom and Gomorrah like the garden of the Lord (Genesis 13:10). Gomorrah, a garden of the Lord? Really, Lot? But how can you blame him when he didn't have that personal connection to the Lord? Lot lived off Abraham's relationship with God. He wasn't connected to God; he was connected to his uncle. Abraham was building his life around God; Lot was building his life around Abraham. Lot had flocks, but Abraham had an altar. Yes, Abraham had flocks, too, but flocks didn't have him. Abraham's possessions didn't possess him. God was his goal. Lot had herds, but no fire. Sadly, he lost everything in the fire of God's judgment. Remember, tents don't last; altars do.

When you have an altar, you're not desperately trying to hold on to people who leave you; you let them go. It's not that you don't care about people; you love them when they come and love them when they go. Yet, your future is not connected to those who leave you, but to God, who stays with you. If you don't have an altar, you might hold on to the wrong people who will end up holding you back from God's purpose. When you don't have an altar in your life, you will be chasing people God is trying to remove from your life. Lot was a veil in Abraham's life. It was after Lot left that Abraham could see the Promised Land God had told him about.

Not holding on to people too tightly is an important part of following God. Jacob couldn't become a nation until he left Laban. Moses couldn't deliver a nation until he left Jethro. God didn't use Gideon until a huge army was sent home. Joshua didn't enter the Promised Land until Moses died. Milk and honey didn't come until manna ceased. Sometimes, before we move into a new season, God moves people out of our lives. If we hold on to the wrong people, they will hold us back from God's purpose. If people want to leave, let them leave. Don't hold on to those who don't want to stay. Don't lose sleep over the people who are not going to be in your future. When people leave, renew your vision and revisit your values. The vision of God's future and the value of God's presence must be a priority.

Let me also say that we should not burn bridges with people who walk away. Moses left Jethro, but Jethro was helpful later on. Lot left Abraham, but Abraham was helpful to Lot in the future.

When Seasons Change

Life is made up of seasons. Seasons change. When seasons change, we have to change our clothing. If we don't change our clothing with the seasons, we will find ourselves burning hot or freezing cold. We don't change with the seasons, but our clothing does. Therefore, it's important that we don't get addicted to positions, titles, and opportunities. We have to work on building the fire in our life so we do not end up chasing after the wind. Seasons change, but our pursuit of God shouldn't; it should remain constant.

A normal year has four seasons: winter, spring, summer, and fall. Joseph, Jacob's son, went through four seasons in his life. These four seasons were reflected in the four seasons of his clothing. While his seasons changed, his commitment to God didn't waver. Dad gave him a colorful coat; his brothers took it away. But they couldn't take away God's presence from his life. Potiphar gave him slave's clothing, Potiphar's wife ripped them off, but she couldn't take God's presence from his life. Then, jail personnel gave him a new set of clothing, and even those he had to leave behind when he went to Pharaoh. Joseph's clothes changed, but his pursuit of God didn't. People can take your title, but they can't take your prayer life. Critics can tarnish your reputation, but they can't steal your character. Someone can ruin your life, but they can't take your fire.

We should be as attached to our positions, titles, and influence as we are to our clothing. When seasons change, clothing changes. Some things go in the closet, others go to Goodwill.

We must not be too attached to the temporal; we should stay addicted to the eternal. If we are not addicted to God, we get too quickly attached to stuff. I learned earlier in life to not get attached to any particular season. Bad seasons don't last. Good seasons don't last, either. Sometimes, God sends you a brook, and as the season passes, it dries up. He gives you manna, and as the season passes, it stops. You have to learn to pivot, not get stuck in one season and die. Build an altar. When you have a prayer life, you learn to pivot. Pray and pivot. Sometimes, God takes away the good to make room for something better in your life. Don't hold on to what's gone and miss what's about to come.

Seasons change. People leave. God remains the same. When you have survived the storm and the shipwreck, build your fire. Our priorities should stay in order. An altar must be permanent. Fire must be built. Your relationship with the Lord must take precedence over everything else.

First Love

Your priorities reveal your passion. Lack of passion for Jesus is a result of misplaced priorities. Jesus rebuked the Church of Ephesus for not having the love for Him that they had at first: "Nevertheless I have this against you, that you have left your first love" (Revelation 2:4). This church didn't lack activities, programs, and busyness. In fact, Jesus complimented the church for her works and the church's ability to spot fake apostles. But the most important thing stopped being the most important thing: They lost their first love for Jesus. They labored for Him but didn't love Him. They ministered *for* the Lord but didn't minister *to* the Lord. What they did for God became so important that they didn't have time for Him.

The word *first* in Revelation 2:4 is the Greek word *prōtos*, which means first in time, in place, in any succession of things or person.[5] Therefore, the first love Jesus refers to is exclusive love that has first place in our hearts, above all else.

The first love we had for the Lord was the result of putting Him first. You can't get the first love without putting Jesus first in your day, week, life, and finances. That's why it's called *first love*. If He is not first, we lose the love we had at first.

Jesus' solution to those who have lost their first love is simple: Remember, repent, and repeat (Revelation 2:5). Remember how things used to be. Repent for not putting Jesus first. Repeat or do the work you did at first. Priorities fuel passion. To get passion for God, we must make God priority number one.

First love is a result of putting Jesus first. It's impossible to burn for the Lord while having messed up priorities. It's impossible to burn for the Lord while waking up to the TikTok feed instead of being fed with God's Word. It's impossible to burn for the Lord if, instead of gathering the daily manna of God's Word, we catch up on the news; if we sleep in on Sunday to watch football instead of going to church; if we immediately pay all our bills instead of first honoring God with our finances. When we start making Jesus our number one priority, passion for Him will flow.

In the Beginning

It's not that God doesn't want us to give attention to our family, have financial savings, and have a professional career. It's just that everything else in our life should not exceed our love for God. He must be first. From the first verse in the Bible, we see that.

In the beginning God created the heavens and the earth.
(Genesis 1:1)

Let me repeat: *In the beginning, God*—God wants to be in our every beginning. He is worthy of being our first. Think back to when Abel offered the firstborn of his flock and was accepted by God (Genesis 4:4). God struck down all the firstborn in the land of Egypt with the last plague, both human and animals, and then He commanded Israel to give their firstborn back to Him (Exodus 13:2; Numbers 3:13). The Lord even told His people to bring the firstfruits of their fruits, grain, olive, wine, and fleece (Exodus 22:29; 2 Chronicles 31:5; Nehemiah 10:35). Jericho was the first city in Canaan that Israel conquered, so guess what? God wanted Israel to dedicate that to Him (Joshua 6:18-19).

You get the idea. God wants the first! He deserves to be the most important priority in our life. There's a story in the Gospels about when someone desired to follow Jesus but first wanted to go and bury his father. Jesus rebuked him (Luke 9:59-60). It isn't that Jesus doesn't value family; He doesn't want to be our second priority in life.

We are invited to seek first the kingdom of God (Matthew 6:33). Some people think they can't seek God's kingdom because they have other responsibilities in life. It's all about who you seek first. Pause for a moment and think about your life as it is now. What do you chase first? Who is the first? Are you building a fire on the island or rebuilding the ship?

Adrian Rogers, an influential Christian leader, once said, "Modern Americans put things first and God second." Ouch! This isn't only true of Americans; it applies to most of humanity. Many love to put things first and God second. We seek after things just as the world does, and those things we seek seem to fly away from us. And God doesn't seem to help us to catch them. All other pursuits don't yield the same results. Jesus said that if we seek Him first, all other things will be added to us (Matt. 6:33). If we pursue God instead of things, things get added. If we put things first, we will miss God. If we put God first, God throws things in as a bonus. So how do we put God first in our life?

Put God First in Your Day

Start your day with prayer. And start your prayer with thanksgiving. Paul told young pastor Timothy, "...first of all that prayers and thanksgiving be offered for all men" (1 Timothy 2:1). I know it's so simple, but how many people actually do it? Putting God first is taking time every day to pray and read the Word. Spending time with the Lord every day is like gathering heavenly manna.

God gave Israel manna to be gathered in the morning as their food (Exodus 16:11-12,15). They had to gather it every day except Saturday. God's Word is our spiritual food to sustain our life. Remember, the Word we received yesterday is insufficient to meet the challenges of the new day. We must have fresh experiences in the Word to keep ourselves alive spiritually. Manna was to be eaten throughout Israel's wilderness wanderings (Exodus 16:35). In the same way, as long as we are living on this planet, we need the heavenly manna. When we get to heaven, the need for it will cease. The Israelites experienced a miracle of manna every day. Sadly, they became complacent and took it for granted; they even despised it (Numbers 11:4-6; 21:5-6). They wanted something more exciting. May we never take God's Word for granted in our lives. May we never outgrow our need for daily fellowship with the Lord.

Gather your manna daily. Wake up a little early to spend time in God's Word and prayer. Jesus did it; He prayed early in the morning (Mark 1:35). The psalmist encouraged an early morning encounter with God (Psalm 5:1-3; 88:13; 119:147). Many men of God spoke about prioritizing prayer in the early morning. E. M. Bounds, the 19th century theologian, said,

> "The men who have done the most for God in this world have been early on their knees. He who fritters away the early morning, its opportunity and freshness, in other pursuits than seeking God will make poor headway seeking him the rest of the day. If God is not first in our thoughts and efforts in the morning, he will be in the last place the remainder of the day."

John Bunyan, the author of *Pilgrim's Progress*, said,

> "He who runs from God in the morning will hardly find him at the close of the day; nor will he who begins with the world and the vanities thereof, in the first place, be very capable of walking with God all the day after. It is he who finds God in his closet that will carry the savor of him into his house, his shop, and his more open conversation."[6]

Now, this doesn't mean that prayer in the evening, or noon, or throughout the day is not something that God hears. We must remain in constant communion with the Lord; however, developing a habit of putting God first by spending your first waking moments in prayer and the Word is one of the best ways to build an altar in your day. Give God your best and He will bless the rest.

Putting God First in Finances

Solomon instructed us to honor the Lord with the firstfruits of all our increase (Proverbs 3:9). Again, it's about honoring God by giving Him His proper place, not just in our calendar but also in our wallet. That's why, as Christians, we give to God first. We gather on Sunday, the first day of the week. We take the first hours or minutes of each day to spend time with Him. It's about priority.

Not all things have the same priority in our life. Sometimes, we give too much attention to the things that scream the loudest. Most people live according to their clock instead of their compass. The clock represents our time; the compass represents our values. We often prioritize what's most urgent in our lives, and wind up sacrificing what's most important.

When it comes to finances, we put God first by giving our first. Abraham practiced that five hundred years before the law of Moses, and we call it tithing (Genesis 14:20). Jacob's grandson promised to tithe to God once he got on his feet (Genesis 28:22). Soon, tithing became law, but that law really had 10% to fund the Levite priest ministry (Numbers 18:21), plus an additional 10% to pay for festivals to build community and celebration (Deuteronomy 14:22-26) and another ten percent every three years to give to the poor (Deuteronomy 14:28-29). Total giving was about twenty-three percent. This is what Israel was required to bring to God. As people under the New Covenant, we don't *have* to tithe; we *get* to tithe. For us, it's not about the law; it's accepting discipline. It's the principle of putting God first in our finances. Jesus didn't reject the law of tithing, but He did correct the Pharisees' overemphasis on minor things at the expense of justice, mercy, and faith (Matthew 23:23).

Tithing is about bringing to God's house the first ten percent of your income. It's a good place to start putting God first. The number ten in the Bible speaks of testing. Tithing is the only practice where God invites you to test Him (Malachi 3:10), but it's also a test of your priorities. When you don't tithe, you rob God of the opportunity to bless you and be involved in your finances. Just as praying early in the day invites God's grace into the rest of your day, so giving your first ten percent invite God's blessing on the rest.

Putting God First Every Week

Luke, in the book of Acts, wrote that on the first day of the week, disciples would gather to break bread (Acts 20:7). The first day of the week is Sunday. On the first day of the week, God separated the light from darkness (Genesis 1:5). We gather on the first day of the week to celebrate the light of Jesus, who has separated us from the darkness. Jesus rose on the first day of the week, which was Sunday (Mark 16:9). The Holy Spirit was also poured out on Sunday (Acts 2:1). In the book of Revelation, Sunday was called "The Lord's Day" (1:10). For Jewish people Saturday was a day of rest, but for Christians, Sunday was the Lord's Day. For Christians, Sunday didn't replace Saturday. At the time, Sunday was like our Monday. It was the day everyone returned to work after a day off. Consequently, the early Church would have likely had to gather for worship either in the morning or evening. This remained the case until Emperor Constantine instituted Sunday as an official day of rest in A.D. 321. But for the early Church, Sunday was a day devoted primarily for worship, not rest.

Put God first every week by going to church. Don't hide behind the excuse, "I don't go to church; I am the church."

That technically and theologically is not correct. Church, from the Greek word *ekklēsia*, means an assembly.[7] It's a gathering of citizens called out from their homes into some public place. A local church is an assembly. The body of Christ doesn't consist of one part; it's made of many parts (1 Corinthians 12:12). You yourself don't make up the church in its entirety. It's us being together as believers that makes up the body of Christ. Therefore, we must gather together. If a local church never meets, it is not a church at all. The meeting isn't just something we do; it's what church is.

God has saved us as individuals to be a corporate assembly. God says in His Word that we should attend church regularly (Hebrews 10:25) Don't allow church hurt to keep you from gathering. Don't allow the devil to keep you from going to church. Don't allow the government to keep you from going to church. Don't allow laziness to keep you from going to church.

Keeping your spiritual fire burning requires, first of all, that you build a fire. In the book of Revelation, God warned the Church of Ephesus to return to the zealous, fervent love they had when they first got saved (2:4-5). God is tired of passive Christianity. Michal, King Saul's daughter, was only a passive window-watcher who sat watching excited worshippers and criticizing them. Regardless of whatever has happened to you in the past, don't let memories of your losses quench your fire for God. Offer up to God your burning, fervent sacrifices of praise on the altar of your heart. Put God first in your life and keep Him there. Put God in first place every day in adoration and prayer and renew your fires among fellow believers on the first day of every week—Sunday. Excuses are a fire extinguisher. Don't let the distractions of life snuff out your fire.

CHAPTER 6

Extinguish Excuses

W hen I was a young youth leader, only about sixteen or seventeen years old, our church was very grateful to the Desert Streams Church for generously allowing us to use their facility on Wednesday nights for prayer and on Thursday nights for our youth service. Because we weren't adults, we weren't privileged to have keys to the building. In one season, my cousin Ilya and I had a radical idea to hold a Friday night prayer vigil. We had heard that churches that have revivals worldwide also have all-night prayer meetings on Fridays. We didn't have the courage to ask the church we rented from to let us pray all night, fearing they would tell us to pray at home. So, we came up with a plan.

The next time we had our Thursday night youth meeting, we sneaked into one of the offices and left an outside window unlocked. The church didn't have security cameras or a security system, so this helped our cause. Then the next night, when everyone was asleep, we would sneak out of our houses, go to a 7-11 store for some caffeinated drinks, and head to church to pray. But there was still one more challenge ahead of us. Getting out of our house wasn't hard to do, but getting into the church undetected wasn't easy because the pastor lived next door. The church had a gravel parking lot and you could hear a car driving in. All he'd have to do was to open his curtains, see our car in the church parking lot, and then come searching for thieves. So, my cousin would turn off the ignition, put the car in neutral, and let the car roll slowly behind the church garbage bin so it would not be visible to the pastor. Then, quietly, we'd break into the church through one of the windows we had left unlocked. We would worship, pray, intercede, and sometimes even doze off a little, and we did this several Fridays and got away with it. However, one night, while praying downstairs, we heard someone walking upstairs and shouting, "Is someone there?!" "Come out, or I will call the police!"

Those steps got louder as the person started to go from the upstairs sanctuary to the downstairs prayer room where we were. We got scared, quickly turned off the lights, and hid under the chairs. It was the church's pastor who lived next door. Thankfully, he never found us and didn't call the police. I told him many years later that we were the ones hiding in his church and I offered an official apology. We laughed together, remembering the good old days. Although I am not proud of breaking into the church, I am indeed grateful for sincerely wanting to pray all night as a teenager, and for discovering a way to do just that. I was determined from a young age to build a fire in my life; I would live in such a way that I wouldn't have to make excuses for why I was not praying, fasting, or reading the Word.

So many people make excuses instead of making a fire. Excuses extinguish your fire. They are like firefighters; they put out your flame. If you want to burn for God, learn to overcome excuses.

Excuses Extinguished

The apostle Paul, a prisoner for Christ, survived the storm and the shipwreck. Finally, he reached the island shore, and it was still pouring down rain. I'm sure cold rain is not as bad as a horrific fourteen-day storm and disastrous shipwreck, but when you're shivering in wet clothes and you don't have a warm house to shelter in, it really does affect you. In Paul's case, with the help of the locals, they started to build a bonfire. Notice that the rain didn't stop them. The cold didn't stop them. Their goal was to build a fire, which was their only means of getting warm in the dark, chilly weather.

You might be thinking, *I get it, Vlad. You say I have to build a fire, but you don't understand my situation. I have been through a terrible storm. I'm not sure if I have strength to build a fire again.* Remember, you can't build a fire as long as you are making excuses. I am here to challenge you to build a fire, not excuses. Remember, excuses are fire extinguishers. Allow me to be completely honest: The storm is not your problem, your excuses are! Whatever pretext you may have, excuses are self-imposed roadblocks that keep you from growing in Christ. It's so much easier to make excuses than to work up the energy to make a fire. When you believe in your excuses, you invite a firefighter into your life. Excuses will extinguish your flame.

Perhaps you're reading this book and your excuse might not be a storm, but a success. You're not bleeding; you're simply too busy. You are not hurting; you're actually pretty satisfied. You might fully believe that you don't need to build a fire because your life is comfortable. Remember that a blessing is not only a reward, but it's also a test. Jesus shared a powerful story about a king who invited guests to the wedding feast, "But they all with one accord began to make excuses" (Luke 14:18). Their excuses for not coming weren't problems or sins, but the "blessings" of their prosperity they were too busy managing.

The rich young ruler's excuse for not following Jesus was that of having too much money; it wasn't a miserable circumstance he was enduring (Luke 18:18-30). Whatever the excuse—storm or success—it must be challenged and overcome. You can only burn for God to the extent that you are able to overcome excuses. Read that again. Living on fire for God is not a result of a personality trait or something you were born with. It's your ability to eliminate excuses. If you overcome excuses, you will want to build a fire.

Let's look at a few excuses that the enemy uses to keep us from building our fire.

"Oh, but it's raining."

A common excuse I've heard is, "I can't build a fire because it's raining." In other words, "I can't pursue God because I'm struggling with sin, bad habits, wrong thoughts, serious problems, abuse, bills, etc. It's raining so hard in my life that I just can't build a fire. The rain will put out the fire." I find it interesting that Paul built a fire during the rainstorm and the cold weather; even the wood he used was soaking wet! I want to emphasize that it is not biblical to think you can get your life right and burn for God simply by believing. The apostle Paul wrote:

I say then: Walk in the Spirit, and you shall not fulfill the lust of the flesh.

(Galatians 5:16)

Notice that he didn't say, "Don't fulfill the lust of the flesh so you can walk in the Holy Spirit." You must walk with the Holy Spirit in order to live a holy life. Where there's no Holy Spirit, there's no holiness. In other words, building a fire of love for Him is the only way to beat your sins and bad habits.

The great D.L. Moody once asked his students,

> "How do you remove air from a drinking glass?" They suggested to use a vacuum or blow the air out. He replied, "The best way to remove the air out of the glass is to fill it with water. The water will push the air out."

The same principle applies to our fleshly desires. We overcome them by being filled with the Spirit and walking in the Spirit.

You must build a fire in spite of rainy weather, even when you don't feel like it. Feed your passion and devotion to the Holy Spirit. If you're addicted, still pray; if you're struggling with sin, still fast; if you're bound by chains, still go to church. This is not a license to keep on sinning; it's an invitation to find the total freedom that is only available in Jesus.

One day a woman who had been bound for 18 years by a spirit of infirmity came to the synagogue (Luke 13:16). She didn't let that spirit of sickness keep her from meeting with God's people. She pushed herself; that disabling spirit didn't stop her from going to church. She took that demon to church with her! In that gathering of believers, Jesus healed her. If she had yielded to the excuse and said to herself, *I am too sick, too bent, too weird to go to church,* she would have missed her miracle that day.

In another instance, there was a man with a legion of demons who ran to Jesus and worshipped Him (Mark 5:6). Think of this: This guy had severe demons manifesting superhuman strength and he was living in a cemetery among tombstones, crying out at night, and running around naked. What? Running up to Jesus and worshipping Him? Maybe he should have gotten his life cleaned up a bit first. Maybe he should have at least gotten dressed. Maybe he should have seen a therapist or a counselor. In other words, it was raining hard in his life; not the best time to build a fire. Yet, he still ran to Jesus and worshipped. The multitude of demons in him didn't like it, but they couldn't stop him. He was determined! And going to Jesus while he was in that situation is how he found his rescue.

Don't let the devil use your struggle as an excuse for why you can't run after Jesus. Don't let the enemy postpone your pursuit of the Lord until a better time, when you might be holier and more righteous. Your time is now!

We become pure through our pursuit of the Lord. No one cleans a dirty window with a dirty rag. No one gets a haircut before going to a barber. "Walk in the Spirit and you will not fulfill the lust of the flesh" means precisely what it says. We must practice walking with the Lord, and then we will not fulfill the lust of the flesh. We can't overcome by our own efforts. We need help, and it comes from Him.

If you can't run after the Lord because of your struggles with sin, walk to Him. When Jesus raised Lazarus from the dead, He commanded him with a loud voice to come out of the tomb or burial chamber (John 11:43). Lazarus got up and walked out of the tomb, still wrapped up with long strips of cloth (grave clothes) from head to toe. He walked out. He probably had to hop out, but he sure enough didn't stay in his tomb. A tomb is where dead people stay and Lazarus wasn't dead anymore. However, he was still wearing a dead man's clothes, which restricted him. You might notice that Jesus didn't send someone inside the tomb to loosen Lazarus. It was only when Lazarus came out to meet the Lord (his best friend) that others came to help him be free. Don't let your grave clothes keep you from walking to the Lord. Don't let your sin keep you from coming to Jesus. Don't let all the rain, your difficult problems in life, keep you from building your fire.

Furthermore, I want you to carefully consider what the Bible does not say. It doesn't say, "Walk in the Holy Spirit, and you will not *feel* the lust of the flesh." Some people get to the point of arrogance and pride as though they are above the Scriptures, above temptation, no longer human. Walking with God doesn't remove temptation; it empowers us to resist stumbling and sinning. Building our fire may not stop the rain, but it sure will keep us warm so we don't die from the cold outside elements. Pursuing God doesn't remove the lust of the flesh, but it gives us the power not to fulfill its demands. All flesh has lusts. Lust has an insatiable appetite; if you feed it, it only craves more. Lust is like athlete's foot fungus—the more you scratch it, the more it itches. God doesn't promise that if you build a fire, the flesh will no longer "itch," but you will have the power to not scratch what is itching. You will have the strength to crucify your cravings instead of satisfying the demands of the flesh.

If you're really dealing with some kind of cold rain in your spiritual life, experiencing constant attacks in your dreams, or falling into the same pattern of sin, don't listen to the devil's lies. He desperately wants you to stop reading the Bible, praying, fasting, and attending church. He will say you're just a hypocrite;

it's not worth your efforts. Remember, sick people go to hospitals. Overweight people go to the gym. Broken people go to God. Don't let your struggles hold you back from going to the Lord. Build your fire, not excuses.

"But I'm just too busy."

Busyness is another excuse for smothering the fire. Martha's busyness with serving her guests distracted her from sitting at the feet of Jesus and hearing His words (Luke 10:40-42). The apostles had to pull back from serving tables when their ministry exploded and retreat to prayer and the ministry of the Word (Acts 6:4). Sin brings us guilt and then becomes a reason why we don't go to God, but busyness makes us feel like we are doing something important for God so He can bless us. Anytime ministry *for* the Lord gets in the way of ministry *to* the Lord, we are in dangerous territory. For us, our labor for the Lord becomes more important than our love for Him. Work becomes our identity. We become human doings instead of human beings. We run faster than God's grace can sustain us. We live our lives being overwhelmed instead of living out of the overflow. Our families get the scraps while we try to give everything to ministry, falsely comforting ourselves that God will take care of our family as long as we are on the ministry treadmill, running non-stop. Busyness steals our fire and it does not add to our productivity. Remember, we are only branches; our abounding comes from our abiding in the vine, Jesus (John 15:5). Our success doesn't come from our efforts, but from our abiding in Him, by "walking in the Spirit." Busyness reduces us to machines that only perform work and never rest. Even if we do produce results, we risk losing our fire.

There were two queens in the Book of Esther. Queen Vashti was busy with the women visitors who had arrived at the palace. Because of this, she didn't come to the king when he requested her. Though we are not given specifics on what the king was planning to do with her in front of his men while drunk, she just didn't come. She was busy serving the women. As a result of her busyness, she lost her crown and probably became a concubine. She most likely still lived in the palace, but she didn't live in the presence of the king. Queen Esther later took Queen Vashti's place. At one point, even though she wasn't invited to go into the throne room to see the king, she went anyway.

- Vashti prepared a feast for women; Esther prepared a feast for the king.
- Vashti was too busy to come when she was commanded; Esther came when she wasn't invited.
- Vashti lost her crown; Esther saved her nation.
- Vashti was into feasting; Esther was into fasting.

I wonder how many times we, as the bride of Christ, live more like Vashti—busy with programs, schedules, responsibilities, and other good things, but we don't take time for the King when He commands us to come. The result? We don't lose our status as a bride, but we lose our intimacy, and just as our intimacy with the King goes, so goes our influence in the spirit realm.

It's okay for us to do things, as long as we are ministering to the Lord in prayer and meditation. Our relationship with Him—receiving from Him and loving Him—needs to be our number one priority. But when busyness steals our fire and zeal, we can freeze to death due to our lack of intimacy with God. It's only when we have our fire burning for the Lord that He will help us to keep a pace of grace in our lives. The pace of our life will carry a sense of His grace. Jesus lived in that pace. He spent nights and early mornings with the Father. Therefore, He wasn't busy; He was simply present with the Father. He didn't run; He walked. He didn't use a fast animal to ride on; He walked. He had the world to save, yet there was a peace about Him. You'd think He would have been stressed, anxious, and overwhelmed, but He wasn't. In fact, He is called the Prince of Peace.

The presence of God gives us a pace where we find peace. Think of this: Jesus walked so slowly that hurting people could touch Him. Never in a hurry, running from one meeting to another. He was always present with His Father every day of the year. Without that kind of intimacy, we are busy, not present with God, running on the performance treadmill but not getting anywhere. Sadly, we can end up outrunning the pace of God's grace.

One thing that hit me hard in my early days, when my ministry started to explode, was that I became busier and busier. I found it harder to keep my devotional times, and to linger longer in the presence of God. I always had things to do, places to go to, people to meet. I got to the place where I felt like I was performing only to check off a list. Then the Lord corrected my attitude by showing me the root of my problem. He pointed out that I would not be able to prioritize His presence in my life as long as I was seduced by the wrong definition of *success*. My "win," if I can call it that, was to reach the world, utilize my full potential, and die empty. In other words, I wanted to make a great impact on the world for God—that seemed like a good goal to aim for. But that was my problem: God became the means to reach my goal! And I was neglecting my spiritual health and family to achieve that goal. The Lord brought Colossians 1:10 to my attention:

...that you may walk worthy of the Lord, fully pleasing Him, being fruitful in every good work and increasing in the knowledge of God.

The part about "fully pleasing Him" hit me hard. The Lord reminded me that Jesus didn't live His life on earth to try to reach the world or even to save everyone by preaching to as many people as possible. He simply obeyed His Father's instructions. He was pleasing to His Father. His death on the cross was part of that obedience to His Father. He died very young. In fact, the results at the end of His life don't seem super appealing to a person who judges by physical metrics or checkmarks. Yet, Jesus said at the end of His life that He had finished completely all the work the Father had given Him to do. How can that be? The Father was pleased with what Jesus did.

Well, I changed my goal after this revelation. My goal now is to please God and Him only! Yes, I do want to reach the world and utilize my potential, but that's not my primary aim. I need to stay on my knees to reflect on how well I am moving toward my ultimate goal. Is God pleased with me? Am I doing what He called me to do? I'm not pleasing God if I am competing with others, and even if I am well known or successful in the eyes of man. I now fight busyness by going to the root of the problem; that's the definition of success.

Unmet Expectations

Another excuse that people often use to not build up their fire is disappointment. What they had hoped for, believed for, fasted for, and prayed for didn't happen. Such unmet expectations become a breeding ground for offense (a "fence") with God, which extinguishes their spiritual flame. It's like water poured out on their fire. Solomon said,

Hope deferred makes the heart sick, but when the
desire comes, it is a tree of life.

(Proverbs 13:12)

The two disciples who were walking on the road to Emmaus felt that way too. They were so disappointed at the outcome of all the events the weekend Jesus died. They said,

But we were hoping that it was He who was going
to redeem Israel.

(Luke 24:21)

Their Messianic hopes had been stirred, but the dream of a liberated Israel died with Jesus. Everyone who has walked with the Lord has experienced this at some time or another. No matter how much faith you have and how much you fast and pray, some things just don't go the way you hope. Other things take longer to develop than you had planned for. Instead of building a fire, some people build an offense against God.

Mary, Martha, and Lazarus were Jesus' friends. However, in John 11, when Lazarus got sick, Jesus didn't run quickly to heal Him. I'm pretty sure the sisters thought that since they were such close friends, they would get special treatment. Isn't that one of the benefits of close friendship? But Jesus came late. It was so late that Lazarus had already died; they had held his funeral four days earlier. That sure didn't meet the sisters' expectations, nor was it an answer to their prayers.

How many times have we found ourselves in the same place? We work at developing a closer relationship with the Lord, which then fuels our faith that all our prayers will be answered. And then, whenever prayer doesn't get answered, it throws us off balance. We wonder, *What's the point of all my praying, fasting, giving, and serving?* Don't get me wrong, we don't serve God in order to get something from Him, but it still hits home when life gets tough and it seems like He is ignoring us.

Mary and Martha were asking for the healing of their brother, but they didn't get a healing. Instead, they got a resurrection. Jesus didn't meet their expectations; He exceeded them! I know that not every story will have a happy ending like this on this side of heaven. But we must rest assured in God's character, that He is good even when everything around us is not.

When I was younger, the source of my disappointment was always seeing others get a breakthrough before I did, especially those who, in my eyes, didn't seem to be paying the price. It felt so unfair. For me, it started with receiving the gift of tongues. I remember when my pastor gathered all of us teenagers to pray to get filled with the Spirit and to speak in tongues. I was devoted to the Lord, and really believed I was more devoted than the others. Because of my devotion, I was expecting that I would get that gift immediately. I don't know if it was self-righteousness or a bit of spiritual pride, but everyone else started speaking in tongues except me. It was disappointing and humiliating. But I decided not to be offended. I went hard after the Lord, praying and fasting every week to position myself to receive that gift. Knowing what I know now, it's a gift I didn't need to strive for; I could have just received it by faith. Although I lacked in understanding, I didn't lack in passion. So, I developed the habit of fasting, and after six months of diligently pursuing the Lord, living waters gushed out of my belly on the balcony of my parent's duplex one Saturday afternoon. I got the gift way later than the others, but in the process, God developed in me a lifestyle of prayer and fasting. I wanted tongues, but God wanted to develop a habit of prayer and fasting in me.

One day when Jairus, the ruler of the synagogue, came running to Jesus, begging him to heal his daughter, Jesus went with him to his house. But, on the way to performing the healing miracle for the girl, someone else interrupted Jesus and got a miracle simply by touching His clothes. It was the woman with an issue of blood. She didn't ask, beg, or plead; she simply touched. Jesus didn't even walk to her house; it happened instantly! Jairus' miracle included walking back to his home with Jesus, but this woman's miracle happened with one touch (Luke 8:40-50). Sometimes, that's how the Lord works. Some get a breakthrough with a simple touch; for others, it takes a walk of faith. Don't get jealous of someone who gets with a touch what requires time for you. Refuse to be offended at God if it takes you longer to get what seems to come so quickly for someone else. Hagar got pregnant quickly and naturally but, for Sarah it took many years and a lot of faith (Genesis 16). And, Hagar wasn't even in a covenant relationship with God!

Pharoah's chief butler got out of prison right after having a dream which Joseph interpreted, but Joseph had to wait for almost two decades before all his dreams came true. He was even stuck in that same prison for a few more years before he was released and his dreams came true (Genesis 40-47). This gets frustrating, disappointing, and at times heartbreaking. This process is painful but necessary because so often, the Lord allows disappointments to purge our motives. God doesn't like to be used. We can't use Him. Jesus has to be our goal, not a means to a goal. If it's all about our miracle, then our breakthrough can become an idol and a distraction.

For the ruler of the synagogue, Jairus, his disappointment was probably not only in the fact that Jesus delayed coming to his house when He stopped for a woman to be healed, (after all, she had no appointment to see Him), but due to this delay, things got even worse at home. Jairus had come for his daughter's healing, not to witness someone else's healing! And while this woman was being healed, his daughter went from being sick to dead. Jairus heard the report that his baby girl had died, even as he was walking with Jesus. It's possible to walk with the Lord and have our circumstances get worse, not better.

This was certainly true in Joseph's case. He went from being hated by his brothers, to being sold, to being made a slave, to being falsely accused, to being imprisoned. And all this happened while he walked in the fear of God. Ouch! Paul went from prison to a shipwreck, a storm, rain, and cold; things just kept getting worse even while he was serving God. That's disappointing. This is never a fun process, but it doesn't have to kill our fire.

I find comfort in the words Jesus spoke to Jairus. When Jairus' heard the news that his daughter had died, Scripture says, "As soon as Jesus heard the word that was spoken, He said to the ruler of the synagogue, 'Do not be afraid; only believe'" (Mark 5:36). That's so awesome. Jesus didn't leave Jairus when things got worse. He just encouraged him to not give up, but believe.

The same Jesus is walking with you. Don't be afraid to keep on walking with Him, even when things get worse. Don't let delay and disappointment kill your fervent devotion, your fire. We don't understand, nor can we see everything that's going on in the unseen spiritual world. Why do some things happen as they do? Why does it take so long?

Think about this: When an archer pulls an arrow backward in the bow, the arrow is not going forward; but it takes being pulled backward to push it forward. When you are going backward and God doesn't seem to meet your expectations, take heart! What if He is planning to exceed those expectations? What if He is setting you up to release you forward? What if, as with

Jairus, Jesus is planning a resurrection? What if you are not being buried, but simply being planted?

Stay close to the Lord. Build a hotter fire. Dig deeper into His Word. Allow your heart to catch on fire so that you will say, like those two disciples, "Did not our heart burn within us while He talked with us on the road, and while He opened the Scriptures to us?" (Luke 24:32). To His disappointed disciples, Jesus explained that there is a process for things—no crown without the Cross, no promise without a process. His divine presence was comforting to them, and their hearts caught fire again.

"Someone hurt my feelings."

A lot of people have trouble moving on after they get their feelings hurt. When we wallow in our hurt feelings, we can quickly become offended with the other person or situation. Offense is dangerous; it is one of Satan's great fire extinguishers. Nazareth was Jesus' hometown but when He showed up in His ministry days, the citizens there were offended. This offense manifested as unbelief and prevented them from receiving Jesus' miracles (Matthew 13:58). Offense blocks our ability to receive from God.

When Jesus was preaching some pretty heavy things, some people couldn't handle the truth and from that time many of His disciples went back and walked with Him no more (John 6:66). Many got offended and left. Jesus mentioned offenses:

> *When Jesus knew in Himself that His disciples complained about this, He said to them, "Does this offend you?"*
>
> (John 6:61)

Taking offense at God will drive you away from Him. Taking offense at others will do the same, driving you away from the Christian community. Offense is the devil's secret weapon to put out your fire for the Lord. The devil often causes offenses to trip us up. One time, Jesus exclaimed,

> *Get behind Me, Satan! You are an offense to Me, for you are not mindful of the things of God, but the things of men.*
>
> (Matthew 16:23)

In my book, *Break Free*, I explained what an offense is:

The most commonly used Greek word for an offense—skandalon—is used in Matthew 18:7. Skandalon is the trigger of a trap, on which the bait is placed. When an animal touches the trigger to eat the bait, the trap springs shut and the animal is caught. An offense is an enticement to a conduct which will ruin the person in question. When my wife and I lived in a duplex, at one point, I saw that we had a mouse in our basement. I cannot stand those little creatures, and the knowledge that they were running around when I slept, gave me the chills. I knew I was not fast enough to catch them with my hands or kill them with a stick. I did what every good homeowner would do—I got into my car, drove to Wal-Mart, and bought some mousetraps. I put bacon and peanut butter as bait on the trap, and I left the trap to work its magic. I would never be able to get rid of the mouse if the mouse would resist the urge to eat bacon and peanut butter.

I never forced it to get to the bait. In fact, I was not present in the house when the mouse got its back snapped by the force of the trigger. That is exactly how the devil works.

You see, he cannot get to us directly, because we are covered by the blood, serving God, and walking in the Spirit. We are annoying to him because we disturb his kingdom and ruin his plans on earth. So, the devil has been using an indirect method to get to us—the best method since the beginning of creation—offense.[8]

Offense is like an automatic weapon which, once you pull the trigger, keeps firing. Offense is usually connected with pride and control. All three operate together as a deadly demonic trio. An offended person can become a control freak. If they can't control a situation or a person, they will leave the church or any other community. Pride comes in as well, and always leads to a fall (Proverbs 16:18). An offended person believes that someone else is to blame rather than themselves. Correction feels like a rejection. Ugliness emerges when someone else injures their pride. Correcting a proud, offended person is like starting an all-out war. They are more concerned with protecting their ego than growing and maturing.

An offended person feels they are owed something. They feel betrayed when they don't receive recognition for their hard work. Think of the older brother in the story of the prodigal son (Luke 15). He is a picture of how offense can destroy your spiritual intimacy with God. When the younger son returned home with a repentant heart, the older brother got offended. No, he wasn't offended that his younger brother came home. He was offended that his father gave the younger brother a party, a young goat, a new set of clothes—all the nice things he felt he himself was entitled to. The older brother had faithfully served his father but never got recognized. He was entitled to everything his little brother, "the loser," got. *It's just not fair!* he screamed within himself. He was so angry and offended that he refused to come into the house. When his loving father came to him, the older son started to vent his offense, accusing his father of ignoring him. For an offended person, it's always everyone else's fault. Sadly, this story ends without us knowing if the older brother repented of his offense or stayed outside in the yard.

There will always be an opportunity to be offended. The devil will make sure of that! There will always be someone who gets something you feel you deserve. Whenever there is an opportunity to be offended, watch out for the trap and its enticing bait. Others don't treat you like you feel you deserve to be treated. People don't compliment your hard work. There will always be someone who will take credit for what you did. While some unfair, unjust things should be addressed, there is something else more important that needs to be dealt with—your heart.

We even harbor silent frustrations with God Himself. All these feelings of being overlooked, ignored, abandoned, or even passed by must be brought to the foot of the Cross. We must love God, not because every dream has come true, but because Jesus bled, died, and rose again so we can be made a new creation in Christ. Respectfully, we must take our eyes off what we think we deserve for all our good works and remember that what we really deserve is to burn in the lake of fire for our sins.

Don't let busyness, disappointment, and offense get you off course. Slow down. Get unbusy by daily walking with Jesus at His pace of living. His grace should be your pace. The devil is after your fire. He uses excuses, life's many complicated problems, your busy schedule, and unanswered prayers to get you to ignore your flame, your fire, your zeal for the Lord. I urge you to stir up the embers. Rekindle the fire the rain has put out. It's so much warmer to stay close to the fire than to shiver in the rain.

CHAPTER 7

Natives Kindled the Fire

Born into a Buddhist family in Pusan, Korea on February 14, 1935, David Yonggi Cho was the oldest of five brothers and four sisters. He graduated from middle school with honors, but his hopes of a university education died when his father's business went bankrupt. He enrolled in a less expensive technical school to learn a trade. Around the same time, he often visited an American army base nearby, and he learned to speak English by befriending soldiers.[9]

When war broke out in Korea during his teenage years, money and food were so scarce that only one small meal a day was common. Malnutrition and unsanitary surroundings in 1953 left him with an enlarged heart condition and tuberculosis invaded his lungs. Sent home to die at the age of seventeen, Cho's father prayed to Buddha, but the young man had little confidence in his father's prayers because he never saw them being answered.

A young woman came to visit Cho's home one day and asked permission to tell the dying teenager about Jesus. Cho ordered her out of his father's house, but she returned for several more days to visit him, each time praying for him despite his cursing and intimidation. On the fifth day, she knelt down to pray for him and began to weep. He was deeply touched and told her, "Don't cry...now I know about your Christian love. Since I am dying, I will become a Christian for you." She gave him her own Bible and said to him, "If you read it faithfully, you will find the words of life." Cho began to cry and said that he wanted to know this Jesus who brought her so often to his home. She left her Bible with him and instructed him to read the story of Jesus in the New Testament Gospels. In his weakened state, one day he walked to an American mission and responded to the call to accept Christ.

His family renounced him as an "unholy Christian dog." However, an American missionary, Louis Richards, took him into his home and began to disciple the dying young man and encouraged him to look to Jesus for total healing. One night while in prayer, Cho had a vision of Christ that overwhelmed him with warm love for the God of his new faith, and this love bubbled up through his mouth, and he began to speak in another language. This frightened him but the missionary explained that this phenomenon was biblical and that many others had also experienced speaking in tongues. While there were still effects in his body from physical weakness, his doctor soon noted that his lungs no longer showed signs of tuberculosis and his heart returned to its normal size.[10]

David Yonggi Cho started the Yoido Full Gospel Church with only five people in a tent meeting, which included his future mother-in-law and her children as its first members. This church became the world's largest congregation with a membership of

830,000 as of 2007.[11] Nobody knows the name of that young lady who sparked a fire in the dying Buddhist teenager, but that spark created a fire which spread throughout the entire nation of South Korea and around the world.

In the previous chapter, we read that after the shipwreck, the apostle Paul and his sailing companions reached the shore of the island on floating boards, where the natives kindled a hot bonfire in spite of the rain and cold wind.

And the natives showed us unusual kindness; for they kindled a fire and made us all welcome, because of the rain that was falling and because of the cold. But when Paul had gathered a bundle of sticks and laid them on the fire, a viper came out because of the heat, and fastened on his hand.

(Acts 28:2-3)

Notice that Paul helped gather sticks to put on that fire, but it was someone else who first got it started! Someone may start a fire in your life, but it will burn hotter with your bundle of sticks. God may use the natives to kindle the fire, but you have a role to play by adding fuel to that flame. Without your help, the fire won't last. Those "natives" can be strangers who witness to you about Jesus. Or maybe you come to the altar and finally surrender at a conference. It could be a church retreat or camp where you encounter God like you never have before. A YouTube video might spark a new passion for God in you. A book you read could light a flame in your soul. Regardless of how your fire starts, you have a role to play. We will talk about this more in the next chapter.

Sparks Start Fires

I recently read about a fifteen-year-old teenager who threw fireworks into the Columbia River Gorge in the state of Oregon, which resulted in 47,000 acres being burned.[12] In 2017, the Eagle Creek Fire smoldered and burned for three months. It even crossed the river into Washington state. In California, a thirteen-year-old girl started the 2014 Cocos Fire, which destroyed thirty-six homes.[13] In another instance, a ten-year-old with matches started the California Buckweed Fire that drove 15,000 from their homes, destroying twenty-one houses and twenty-two buildings.[14] Big fires get started with small sparks. The same is true in the spiritual realm. God sets hearts on fire by using places and people. The burning bush lit Moses on fire, which resulted in the deliverance of a nation. Moses lit Joshua on fire, which led to him conquering the Promised Land. The voice spoken to the child Samuel kindled a flame in him. Samuel lit that fire in young David when he poured oil on his head. Fire fell on 120 disciples in the upper room, sparking a movement that swept across the entire known world. Sometimes, God sparks fire within a person through supernatural visitation. Other times, He uses someone to spark that fire through impartation. Paul had an encounter with Jesus on the road to Damascus, but Timothy received spiritual gifts through Paul laying hands on him. God can choose to kindle your flame directly through supernatural visitations or indirectly through divine impartation.

The natives kindled a fire. Paul simply put an armful of wood on the fire which they had started. God starts the fire; we are responsible for keeping it ablaze.

When I was a teenager, my pastor, who is also my uncle, lit that spark in my soul. He prophetically spoke into my life many, many times that God would use me, and I would reach the world for Jesus. For me, he was that "native" from Ukraine who kindled my flame. I was thirteen years old, insecure, confused, and struggling. It didn't matter that it was raining and cold in my life; he still lit the match to start my fire for the Lord.

When I was about fourteen years old, something happened that I will never forget. I was already preaching weekly; my pastor would have us preach in the morning at our church and then in the evening take us to preach out of town. I joke that my traveling ministry started when I was fourteen. On one of those trips, I spoke at a church in the Seattle area. After a powerful service, an elderly grandma pushed through the crowd, approached me, and grabbed my hand. With piercing eyes and an excited voice, she looked at me and said that during my preaching, she saw a vision of a trumpet on my lips and a fire coming out of the trumpet. This was the first time I ever received a prophecy and vision. It ignited a holy passion in me to wholeheartedly pursue God. Since then, I have received hundreds of prophetic words and visions, but that one in Seattle kindled a flame. I strongly believe the Holy Spirit urgently desires for us to light fires in other people. Prophecy, visions, and dreams are not meant to tickle people's ears but to set them on fire!

Events Lead to Experiences

God encountering you at a church conference, camp, or at the altar can spark a fire that will change the trajectory of your life. I have witnessed it at our conferences: demons coming out of people, the sick being healed, the bound being set free, souls getting saved, believers being revived. These meetings can be like those natives that kindle the fire. But as good as they may be, you can't survive on conferences; they can only spark a fire.

One thing we do during our deliverance services is to ask people to bring to the altar demonic objects and any other items that are destructive. This alone is a powerful act of freedom for many people. I have seen many people set free from drugs and cigarettes as they lay those items on the altar. Significant moments like these are used by God to spark a fire.

Youth camps are places that create divine sparks. Last year, I met a family from another state, whose daughter didn't want anything to do with Christianity. I asked them to send their daughter to our annual youth camp. She came, and on the second night something happened. I was preaching and I saw her receiving the message, taking notes. When the altar call came, she was one of the first people at the altar, weeping uncontrollably, and she ended up speaking in tongues that same night. She returned home as a teenager set on fire. A spark was created at that summer camp.

God does use events, places, and people to kindle a fire. However, revival is not an event, but a lifestyle. Many of us can trace revival in our own life to one specific event. Don't underestimate the importance of revivals, conferences, and camps. Regular church activities, programs and schedules are fine, but once in a while, we need to step out of our predictable, familiar patterns of life. That's where you find sparks flying.

Pay with Attention

We live in a day and age where most of us watch YouTube videos, probably subscribe to a podcast and download a book on tablet or buy one online. Books, podcasts, and YouTube videos can be "natives" that God might use to kindle a fire, but the devil can also use them to put out a fire. It goes both ways. Music, books, and videos are either fire starters or firefighters.

I remember when cassette tapes initially ignited a flame within me concerning the fear of the Lord. I was hungry for a revival, so I tried to feed myself with cassettes on revival. One time I bought a seven-cassette tape series on the Great Argentine Revival. I listened intently to the history of how the Argentine church struggled and eventually they felt God's calling to fervently cry out for revival. It started with many young people who would be so filled with a spirit of intercession that the carpets would be soaked with tears. The glory of God visited that nation. And listening to those tapes sparked within me a desire for intense prayer, which produced conviction of my own sins. I would find myself wailing for hours on the floor, asking God to cleanse my heart. Yes, God can use audio sermons to spark revival.

The Bible says that faith comes by hearing (Romans 10:17). There are things that can come into our life by the ear gate (our ears). Therefore, we must be watchful that the ear gate is open to only things of the Holy Spirit. So many Christians listen to music where the lyrics glorify sex, drugs, gangs, or woke propaganda; and then they wonder why they are struggling with bad habits, cursing, and lustful thoughts. If you really want to burn for God, ask Him to spark the fire through what you listen to. Listening to secular music but trying to live a holy life is like drinking toilet water and yet trying to stay healthy. Let your ear gate be open only to godly music and messages—you will see how that will create a spark. Our culture is dominated by godlessness. The enemy uses music, rhythm, and lyrics to spark and maintain his revival of sin, immorality, and perversion.

Jesus said,

> Take heed what you hear. With the same measure
> you use, it will be measured to you; and to you who
> hear, more will be given.
>
> (Mark 4:24)

Be aware of what you give your attention to, because where you put your attention today will produce your appetite tomorrow. If you want to have an appetite for God, pay close attention to the things of God. Appetite comes from your thoughts and your focus. Your attention is the currency of your spiritual appetite. Today's attention brings tomorrow's appetite. That's why we say in English, "pay attention." You're paying for things you're hungry for with the attention you give to them. Appetites can be a biome or the flora and fauna that are favorable for growing addictions. What you consume today can control you tomorrow.

Examine your attention, your focus, and your heart. Are they causing you peace or anxiety? Are they causing you to burn for God or burning you out? Nurturing you or numbing you? Equipping you or entertaining you? God wants to use your ear gate to bring about changes in your spiritual life—to light a fire in your soul. Would you open that gate to only godly things?

Eyes on Fire

Eyes are also a gateway, but they are the gateway to the soul. There can't be fire in the heart without sparks coming through the eyes. As with the ears, so it is with the eyes. What is the usual way that men and women burn with lust? It starts with the eyes. Samson saw a woman before he slept with her. David saw Bathsheba before he committed adultery with her. Although it was too late, David afterwards resolved to set nothing wicked before his eyes. He knew that he couldn't burn for God in his heart and still allow what he saw to defile him. Job said that he had to put a lock on that gateway of eyes.

I made a covenant with my eyes not to look lustfully...
(Job 31:1 NIV)

Jesus' eyes are full of pure, holy fire. If God is to come and start a fire in your heart, He will be coming through your eye gate. If the devil comes to destroy you, he will try to come through that same gate. Jesus told us,

The eye is the lamp of the body. If your eyes are good, your whole body will be full of light. But if your eyes are bad, your whole body will be full of darkness.
(Matthew 6:22-23 NIV)

One way that holy fire gets kindled in your heart is through reading. First and foremost, that reading should be in God's Word. The Bible is God-breathed (2 Timothy 3:16). This means when you read it, it's like you're enabling God to breathe into your soul. No wonder reading God's Word brings so much benefit, inspiration, encouragement into your life. God said His Word is like fire (Jeremiah 23:29). Reading your Bible ignites a fire, and meditating on it fans the flame. When Jesus spoke to His disciples on the way to Emmaus, their hearts caught fire and their lives were never the same.

And they said to one another, "Did not our heart burn within us while He talked with us on the road, and while He opened the Scriptures to us?

(Luke 24:32)

All Jesus was doing while walking with them was explaining the Scriptures about Himself. The Bible not only became alive, but it kindled a flame in their hearts. God's Word burns with love. It purges sinful thoughts. It lights a fire of godly passion inside you.

Diet Determines Destiny

Reading God's Word allows the fire of God to penetrate through your eyes into your soul. Reading Christian Spirit-filled books can also create a spark. But no book is to ever be valued on the same level as the Holy Bible. Christian books are only supplements, not the source. The Bible is the only source of truth.

I am a huge advocate for Spirit-inspired Christian books. My life has been impacted by them a lot. In my teenage years, when I read the book, *Sex and the Single Soul* by Jack Hayford, a revelation came to me that there must be a demonic spiritual force behind my obsession with pornography. That revelation led me to not only repent sincerely, but also to get engaged in spiritual warfare. This is how I was delivered from pornography. AW Tozer's book, *The Pursuit of God* lit a fire in my soul to fervently seek God above everything else. Andrew Murray's book, *The Vine* taught me to abide in Him. David Yonggi Cho's book, *The Fourth Dimension* taught me the power of a sanctified imagination and how it's connected to faith. Benny Hinn's book, *Good Morning Holy Spirit* showed me that the Holy Spirit is a person. Robert Morris' book, *The Blessed Life* gave me a framework for radical generosity, which is something I continue to practice to this day. Jentezen Franklin's book, *Fasting* put a fire in my heart to fast. Leonard Ravenhill's book, *Why Revival Tarries* put a spark into my life to pray. John Bevere's book, *Under Cover* put a spark in my life to honor authority. Watchman Nee's book, *The Normal Christian Life* put a spark in my heart about my identity. And the list goes on and on.

Reading the Word is like spiritual eating. And if we are what we eat, we also become what we read. Eve ate herself out of paradise (Genesis 3:23). Esau ate himself out of his blessing (Genesis 25:33). You can be in a good place with God, but if you start feeding yourself with spiritual junk food, you will get sick spiritually. You can be in a weak place right now with God, but if you choose to start feeding yourself with fresh spiritual food, you will become stronger. Good books spark spiritual growth. But be careful of what you're reading, because eating the wrong stuff can also make you spiritually sick. Ask God for discernment on what to read.

I recently encountered an awkward situation. My friend pastor Ilya recommended to me some vitamin supplements which are meant to increase cognitive function—to help my brain function even better. My wife ordered some for me. I read the instructions on the label to take two pills a day and I took them. When I did, I suddenly felt like vomiting. I waited for a few days to try them again and I had the same result. I thought maybe something was wrong with my brain. I asked my friend Ilya if he had the same symptoms. He said no. I went back to the bottle and read that these supplements I had been taking for my cognitive function were *for dogs only*. I guess the same company that makes some supplements for humans also makes them for dogs. Interestingly, those supplements wouldn't make a dog sick, but they sure made me sick. Discernment is what's needed so that we don't take "supplements" that are not meant for Christians. Maybe those books and materials are perfect for those who are perishing, but for us who are being saved, they can make us sick. Look for books that bring a spark, not sickness.

Fresh, Fast, and False

When it comes to the type of teaching that we let influence our lives, I want to provide you some insights. We live in a day and age when, if you disagree with a preacher, you might think it makes him a false teacher. Yes, false teachers do exist and the Scriptures warn us about them, but as Christians, we cannot throw the term "false teacher" or "false preacher" around loosely. We should not label someone a false teacher simply because they teach in a style we are not used to or because they wear ripped jeans, have tattoos, and wear earrings. I want to break this topic into three categories that can help you to better understand what characteristics indicate someone is really a false teacher. We will look at "fresh" teaching, "fast-food" teaching, and false teaching.

"Fresh" teaching refers to biblical teachings fresh from God's Word that give new and deeper insights, providing a new look at the old. "Fresh" teaching exalts Jesus with deeper revelations of His nature and character. It might be a book about the power of the Holy Ghost, or an article on prayer which glorifies God. This type of godly teaching is not just motivational or inspirational; it reveals the true, sinful nature of man, the reality that hell is hot, and the redemptive gift that was provided at the Cross.

"Fast-food" teaching focuses primarily on what just makes you feel good. Most of the time, these preachers are more motivational speakers than preachers of the whole Word of God. Honestly, it is not wrong, but it capitalizes on one topic or doctrine over others in Scripture. In Acts 20:27, Paul said, "for I have not shunned to declare to you the whole counsel of God." This indicates that there were (and still are) preachers who did not declare the whole counsel of God. Today we might notice that they preach only eighty percent of the counsel of God as it relates to faith, fasting, prayer, grace, and sin, without touching on subjects like healing, the gifts of the Holy Spirit, and deliverance from demons. Christians sometimes judge those who are "fast-food" preachers and tag them as false teachers simply because they don't preach on all the other topics in the Bible.

Acts 18:24-28 gives an example of the preacher Apollos who was an eloquent man, mighty in the Scriptures, and preached in the pagan city of Ephesus. He was "fervent in spirit, spoke and taught accurately of the things of the Lord, though he knew only the baptism of John." While preaching in the synagogue, Priscilla and Aquila realized Apollos was missing certain things in his teaching, so they pulled him aside. They did this however, not to classify him as a false teacher for only preaching what he understood about the baptism of John, but they "explained to him the way of God more accurately," to bring him into the whole counsel of God.

"False" teaching, which is taught and promoted in videos, podcasts, and books, is something we must avoid. All the New Testament writers dealt with this issue. Peter addressed it in his second letter, highlighting a false teacher as someone who denies Jesus Christ, glories in Christian freedom, but is actually indifferent to their Christian duties (2 Peter 2). This means that there are people who preach that just because one is saved, he can keep on sinning. They often take advantage of their followers in order to enrich themselves. Jesus warned us that false teachers would be known by their fruits (Matthew 7:15-20). They live a compromising life, indulging in sinful practices.

We must learn to grow in discernment. I encourage you to find teaching, preaching, books, and podcasts that will help you grow into a well-rounded man or woman of God. But remember, although it is beneficial to read other books, our primary source of teaching should be the written Word of God. Stay in God's Word. Everything else, like commentaries, dictionaries, sermons on YouTube, and books (including my own) are only a supplement to your spiritual growth. We do not need to depend on additional resources to understand the Bible; we simply need the Holy Spirit to explain what He inspired. Books help, but the Holy Spirit is the greatest teacher.

God Encounters

While it's true that God will use places and people to spark a fire, I don't want to downplay the importance of your personal encounters with God that may change your direction in life. Moses, on the backside of the desert, had a supernatural conversation with God, which altered his course in life. Gideon, while hiding from the Midianites, encountered an angel which changed the rest of his life. God spoke audibly to Paul on the road to Damascus and all the rest is history. Although not everyone's encounter will be as dramatic or similar, God often sparks something through personal, supernatural encounters. Those moments, however brief they may be, form a spiritual momentum that creates a dramatic movement in our life. Encounters with God, whether small or great, will ruin you for "normal." They disrupt your routine. Although routines may be good, they can also keep you stuck in a spiritual rut. God's supernatural visitations, whether in prayer, while reading the Scriptures, and even in dreams or visions, can break you away from the familiar and bring back a holy fascination with God.

Wise men from the east were following a star, seeking the King of the Jews, but when they arrived in Jerusalem, they met religious scholars who already knew where He was supposed to be born. The scribes had all the right information but lacked passion to act on that info and look for the Christ whom they had read about. The wise men sought to see King Jesus. As the famous quote says, "Wise men still seek him." They followed His star, while the scholars just read about Him. And the wise men's seeking wasn't in vain. They encountered Jesus Christ. They didn't just read about Him; they saw Him. It was a simple, but powerful encounter. It released worship and radical generosity from them to the Savior. They didn't go back the same way! Their direction changed.

The reason your encounters with the Lord might seem small, especially if you compare them to someone else's encounters, is because they are only meant to be a spark for you. For as long as I can remember, I wanted to have a powerful encounter with God. I think this desire was rooted in my belief that the greater the encounter with God, the greater the impact my life would have on this world. Honestly, my desire wasn't for God, but for myself. My view changed with time. It became wanting to know God just for knowing God personally, not for what I can get out of Him. I learned that all "God encounters" are like the safety matches that are used to kindle something inflammable, not to be an end in themselves. Encounters are not the ultimate experience; they are steps on a ladder leading upwards.

This is the best way to describe the encounter I had with the Holy Spirit when I was earnestly seeking the gift of speaking in tongues. As I said, an intense hunger for more of God drove me to pray daily and fast weekly. Then, at last, there came a tipping point at 2:00 p.m. on a Saturday afternoon on the balcony of my parents' duplex. I am not sure why I decided to pray on the balcony, but rivers of living water flowed out of me in a way that I had never experienced. A heavenly language flowed out and what a sweet experience that was! My prayer life was changed forever.

Two years later, when I was sixteen, I became the youth leader. The first youth pastor quit after six months, then the second youth pastor quit after six months. I was the third one, and after six months, I decided to quit as well. I wasn't ready for a youth ministry. I wasn't ready to be a leader, nor prepared for this. Mind you, we had only seven young people attending the meetings and most of them were my relatives.

One of the unpleasant youth meetings became the straw that broke the camel's back. I made up my mind to call my uncle, my pastor, and call it quits. But a divine encounter with God changed all of that. On my way home, my family stopped by a grocery store. They went into the store, and I stayed in the car. I broke down in disappointment, feeling defeated. But suddenly I heard the inner voice of God, not audible, but very, very real. This is what I felt He said, "If you don't quit, you will pastor a church where people will come from every nation in the world—the hungry will be fed, the sick will be healed, the demonized will be set free, and the lost will be found." That encouraging word lit a fire in me to serve God. I never did make the call to my pastor about quitting. At sixteen years old, my fire started to burn.

Over the next ten years, I didn't see much progress in my ministry, but I held onto that word, or, I should say, that word held me. I would often visit that place in the grocery store parking lot to be reminded of what God said to me. Today I see happening exactly what God promised me that day in the car. It was that unforgettable encounter that set me on fire for what I am doing today. Sometimes God directly sparks us with a word, a touch, or an experience. Other times it happens indirectly through a book, an event, or a person. The main point is that God sparks us.

One intimate encounter with God will change you, but ongoing encounters with God will change the world around you. One visitation from God can and should lead to ongoing visits with Him. Moses' encounter with God speaking to him in the burning bush on His mountain was just the beginning. He kept going back to His mountain to continue his encounters with the Lord. His first encounter left a mark on his life, but his continuous encounters with the Lord left a mark on the world.

God wants to encounter you and set you on fire! Be open to people whom God sends into your life to get a fire started in your heart. Instead of expecting a big manifestation from an awesome encounter with God, learn to use and develop what God has already given you. Don't compare your experience with someone else's. It's only a spark that God wants to use to create a blaze in your personal life.

And remember, sparks don't last. The natives kindled a bonfire, but the flames constantly required more fuel. Paul gathered an armful of sticks to put on that fire, but more wood was going to be needed. In the next chapter, we will learn why many sparks do not lead to lasting change.

CHAPTER 8

A Bundle of Sticks

When I asked my wife to marry me, I gave her a ring as a token of my love. Our wedding was amazing; at least that's what I thought. I had been saving money for the wedding for a long time and I took pride in the fact that we didn't go into debt. It all looked glorious. My parents were happy, and my bride seemed to be happy, too. But later I found out that my wife didn't like it all that much and I was pretty disappointed. She didn't want so many people she didn't know at the wedding. One of the things we decided to do early in our marriage was to renew our wedding vows every ten years with an actual wedding ceremony. So, ten years after our first wedding (sounds kind of weird), we had our second wedding. This time it was just as my wife wanted—very intimate, close family and friends, in my parents' backyard. Oh, and I also gave her a second wedding ring that was way nicer than the first.

I technically have been married twice to the same person. We didn't have a renewal of our vows because our marriage was struggling, but because we wanted to invest in our relationship. It's one thing to fall in love; it's totally another thing to walk in love. But having a big, fancy wedding ceremony doesn't mean you will have a great marriage.

Although I love to perform and/or attend beautiful wedding ceremonies, I'm more impressed by strong and beautiful marriages. A wedding can be nice because a lot of thought and planning is put into it, but a marriage suffers when spouses get lazy and stop working on it.

My wife and I made a conscious decision that our marriage will always be a top priority, and our ministry will flow out of our marriage. Our marriage will not get the leftovers after ministry. We have done our best to prioritize coffee dates, dinner dates, getaways and vacations but, more important are our daily ten to fifteen minutes of intentional listening.

It's a well-known truth that great marriages don't just happen by accident; they happen on purpose. The same is true with our relationship with God. Having a great start in your walk with God at a conference, camp, or an experience at the altar is like having a great wedding. That's great, but does it translate into a lifestyle of pursuing Him? Revival is not an event; it's a lifestyle. There is a price to pay to walk that out.

So, let's get back to the weddings and rings. Shortly before our tenth anniversary, my wife's first ring went missing. It was after our Philippines ministry trip, just before the Covid pandemic. Lana didn't tell me that the ring was missing, and I didn't notice that she was wearing a different one (jewelry is not my thing). So, we celebrated our tenth anniversary with a new wedding and renewal of our vows and my wife got an upgraded wedding ring.

One year later, we were hosting a Raised to Deliver conference in Vancouver, Washington, and after the conference, as we left the hotel to drive home, Lana panicked. She was missing her new ring. We returned to search the room and the ring was gone. We filed a report and only then did I learn that Lana was missing both rings now, the first one after the Philippines trip and now the second one after a successful conference. Let's just say I wasn't super happy. Of course, I was looking for someone to blame. At first, I blamed my wife and was upset with her that she was losing her wedding rings. I said, "No more rings." I reminded her that my traditional Pentecostal roots didn't even allow for jewelry, so maybe I should revert to that. Of course, I was upset. My wife admitted that she had lost the first ring, but the second one had been stolen. A few years later, we did find the first ring in a drawer. But the second one that went missing after the conference is still missing.

I learned a valuable lesson: There is a distinct difference between something being stolen and something that just goes missing. We lose things by negligence, and sometimes we are able to find them later. But when something is stolen, it is always the work of a thief. The devil is a thief and a firefighter in the worst sense. He wants to put out your precious fire. But most of us don't get our fire stolen by the devil—we lose it. The fire just dies out on its own, not because the devil had anything to do with it, but because we failed to keep it burning.

Fire Needs Fuel

But when Paul had gathered a bundle of sticks and laid them on the fire, a viper came out because of the heat and fastened on his hand.

(Acts 28:3)

Paul gathered a bundle of sticks to put them on the fire that the natives kindled. They started it, but he kept it going by putting more wood on it. Fire needs fuel. A spark is enough to start it, but it's not enough to keep it going. Someone must put sticks on that fire, or it will die out. That's why the fire you get at the conference often doesn't last. The spark you receive at a revival service won't last if you don't immediately start putting some wood on it. Many people get on fire but soon lose it, not because the fire wasn't real, but because any fire needs fuel. Instead of gathering sticks, we go from conference to conference seeking a man of God who might be used to kindle your fire again. It's like going from spark to spark, looking for sparks. Natives can kindle it, but you yourself are responsible to gather a bundle of sticks, or else that fire will die.

I've had a front-row seat to watching young people catch on fire at a camp retreat, only to become lukewarm soon afterward. So often, I have seen adults get kindled for the Lord at the altar but fail to carry that fire in their homes. We develop an unhealthy dependence on events, simply because we haven't developed personal altars at home. We begin to live by hype instead of holy habits. We have had powerful moments that don't last. Instead of turning them into momentum that lasts and grows with time, we let them fizzle out.

The Old Testament priests were commanded to keep the fire burning.

> *And the fire on the altar shall be kept burning on it; it shall not be put out. And the priest shall burn wood on it every morning, and lay the burnt offering in order on it.*
>
> (Leviticus 6:12)

I want you to see that God didn't expect the fire to keep on burning without someone putting in some wood on the altar. God may start it, but we must keep it going. Our God who answers by fire also makes His ministers to be a flame of fire.

Staying on fire doesn't happen by accident. Priests had to burn wood every morning. Let me repeat: Bringing wood every morning is what was required for the fire to keep burning.

Israel had seven feasts: Passover, Unleavened Bread, Firstfruits, Pentecost, Trumpets, the Day of Atonement, and Tabernacles. Burning wood only during those feasts wouldn't keep the fire burning on the altar. They had to do it daily, even when the festivities were over. Their feasts were like the special events that we all attend to energize our faith, but they don't sustain our flame. Not only did priests have to bring wood daily, but they also had to offer sacrifices on that altar. If priests stopped putting wood and sacrifices on the altar, the fire would die out. It's not God's responsibility to keep the fire burning, it's the task of the priests.

You are God's priest; in fact, you're part of the royal priesthood (1 Peter 2:9). As God's priest, keep the fire burning on your altar. Your heart is the place where you put fire. It's a place for God's fire. It's not a trashcan of sin for the devil to use. Keep the fire burning on the altar. Gather a bundle of sticks and place it on the altar daily.

Apostle or Apostate

A personal experience with God is a powerful moment like a spark, but if it doesn't lead to you gathering more sticks, that encounter won't bring lasting results. There were two men named Saul in the Bible. Both had incredible experiences with

God. One was a king; the other was a Pharisee. One Saul went to Ramah to catch and kill David; the other Saul went to Damascus to catch and kill Christians. One Saul had an encounter with the raw power of God and ended up unclothed on the ground; the other Saul got hit with the power of Christ and became blind. One Saul momentarily felt bad about what he was doing; the other Saul actually repented. One Saul stopped pursuing David for a short period of time; the other Saul started doing what God wanted him to do right away. One Saul became an apostate; the other Saul became an apostle. Both had experiences, but only one gathered a bundle of sticks to put on that fire for God. King Saul had a real experience in the presence of Samuel and the prophets (1 Samuel 19:23-24), but it didn't lead to a true repentance, a change of mind that should have resulted in a change of his life's direction.

You can start a blazing fire with gasoline or lighter fluid, but it quickly dies out. I want to emphasize this again: Events are not enough. Experiencing God powerfully in one place is not enough; it must blend into a sincere lifestyle of walking together with Him. An encounter must lead to a lifestyle of revival. God wants consistency in our being on fire for Him. Not moments, but momentum. Not just leaps we take, but a lifestyle we maintain. He desires our lamps to be continually burning.

> Yet I hold this against you: You have forsaken
> your first love.
> (Revelation 2:4; also see 3:15-16)

Impartation may give you a spark, but it's the intimacy that keeps that fire going. It's not just about making new promises to do better, but actually developing a personal process of following God daily. Revival is not an event; it's a lifestyle where godly routines are developed.

A Threefold Cord

So, let's gather a bundle of sticks. I want to present to you three disciplines that, if bundled together, will sustain your flame for God. There are three things Jesus told us to do in secret that yield a public reward. This spiritual bundle of sticks includes giving, praying, and fasting. For each of these disciplines, Jesus said a reward will come from the Father if they are done with the right motives (Matthew 6:1-18). If prayer, giving, and fasting are done in secret, they bring about God's open supernatural reward.

This bundle of three spiritual disciplines is also what helps us to fight back against the enemy. Here's devil's deadly trio: pride, greed, and the lust of the flesh. When we combine prayer, giving, and fasting, it's like a spiritual threefold cord. This cord helps you defeat the deadly trio of pride, lust, and greed. Prayer defeats pride. Giving defeats greed. Fasting defeats lust. Solomon tells us that a threefold cord is not easily broken (Ecclesiastes 4:12). When you combine this bundle of three strands—prayer, giving, and fasting—you will not be easily broken. You will easily break the grip of the enemy's plots because these three disciplines bind the flesh. You must bind the flesh before the devil uses the flesh to bind you.

Bind, Build, Breakthrough

Not only do these disciplines bind the flesh, but they also build up your spirit man. Prayer connects you to God. Fasting disconnects you from the natural world. Giving redirects your heart. These three work together in concert to strengthen the spiritual man. It's like a physical fitness gym for your spirit man. When life gets hard, we must get stronger. God doesn't always remove the struggle; He renews your strength. He strengthens your inner man to meet the challenges that come from living in this broken, sinful world. Too many people quit, not because the struggle is too hard, but because their strength is too weak. Instead of feeding the spirit man daily, they are feeding the flesh. No wonder the devil usually gets the upper hand. Start praying, fasting, and giving and you will notice yourself becoming stronger, and the flesh becoming weaker.

A bundle of sticks keeps the fire going. They bind the flesh and build up your spirit. Combined together, prayer, fasting, and giving can also birth supernatural breakthroughs in your life. The Roman commander Cornelius was a great man who practiced a combination of these three habits (Acts 10:1-4). He prayed regularly to God, fasted, and gave alms. And a breakthrough came to his household. One day, God's angel in shining clothes visited Cornelius. In the meantime, Peter was in prayer in another city and the Holy Spirit spoke out loud in a vision, giving Peter instructions and directions to go to Cornelius' house. Peter obeyed and went to visit him in his house. This supernatural encounter made Cornelius, his household, and his close friends to become the first Gentiles (non-Jews) to be saved. His prayers, fasting, and giving did not contribute to his salvation. Our salvation is by grace alone through faith in Jesus Christ. But something broke in his life, in the spiritual realm, through practicing these three things. Even God's angel acknowledged that his prayers and generous gifts to the poor came up before God as a memorial. God took notice of Cornelius because of these practices.

Make prayer, fasting, and generous giving as natural as breakfast, lunch, and dinner. Develop a habit of prayer, the habit of fasting, and a habit of giving to the needy. Don't just do it when you feel like it. Do it to feed the fire. Don't use prayer as a spare tire; make it a daily priority. Don't use fasting only as a response to crisis; make it a regular practice in your walk with God. The same goes for unselfish giving. Don't give just because the preacher is begging for you to give toward a church project. Give because it's the fuel for the fire, the cord to bind up your flesh and build up your spiritual man. Remember, fire is kindled by God, but it will burn hotter with your bundle of sticks. When you combine prayer, fasting, and giving in one bundle, you will feed your passion for God.

Thirty, Sixty, One Hundred

One time, Jesus talked about the parable of a farmer and a field of good, rich soil that produced good fruit. At harvest time, some areas yielded thirty, some sixty, and some even one hundred times more than the sower planted (Matthew 13:8). Keep this parable in mind when it comes to practicing the three disciplines that produce the spiritual fruit of binding the flesh, building up the spirit man, and bringing breakthrough. Naturally, we tend to emphasize one thing over another. For example, some love to pray but don't practice fasting. Others love to fast but are not generous. Others may be generous but neglect prayer, etc.

God wants to build up all three muscles in your spiritual life. If you only do the parts of the Bible that come easy for you, you'll miss the opportunity to bear much fruit. Don't limit your effectiveness in serving the Lord by staying at the 30-fold level, growing only in one area such as prayer. Comfort keeps us from growth. Convenience keeps us from our true calling. Go for the hundredfold blessing by going one-hundred percent in all three areas. In God's Kingdom, we can't get maximum results with minimum inputs. The soil that was good had to be cleared of rocks and thorns. There was a price to be paid. A great and fruitful harvest doesn't just happen by accident.

For me personally, fasting was the easiest when I was younger. I truly looked forward to it and enjoyed a one-day weekly fast and then a three-day fast each month. With time, I developed a strong commitment to early morning prayer and weekly Friday night vigils. But gladly giving money out of my pocket was the hardest thing for me to do. Don't get me wrong; I was a faithful tither, but it took me a while to grow into being generous and sacrificial. And now I would say that, until radical giving became my regular lifestyle, I didn't see all that God promised me. It's like I was operating in the sixtyfold area of my life, not the hundredfold. I noticed that in my ministry, I was not where God wanted me to be. It was like there was a ceiling in the spirit realm. I really wished that the blockage would have been a demon so I could have simply engaged in spiritual warfare and cast it out. It costs me nothing to yell at a demon. In fact, I even increased my prayer and fasting at one time to try to break through to the next level, but God didn't want more prayer and fasting at that time. He wanted my obedience in joyful giving. That obedience was for me to lay on the altar my stinginess, my fear of being overly generous. When I finally did start giving much more than my ten percent tithe, something broke inside me, something broke through in my ministry and in my personal life. I am a witness that when you gather a complete bundle of sticks, you will maintain the fire that God starts.

"Natives" may kindle your fire of zeal, commitment, and love, but you are the one who must gather sticks. God won't do it for you! I can't stress this enough: A conference may start your passion, your "first love" for God, but it's your godly choices that keep it burning. You will not stay on fire unless you consider what you are doing daily. Stay in tune with the Holy Spirit. Repent. Meditate on your Bible. Always keep in mind the three essential things Jesus tells us to do, which God sees and will reward you for by drawing you closer to Himself: prayer, fasting and giving. These three disciplines will enable you to bind the flesh, build up your inner man, and get breakthroughs in life. In the next few chapters, we will take a little time to address them one by one.

CHAPTER 9

The Stick of Prayer

D ave had a rough upbringing. His mother was an alcoholic, and his father was in and out of jail, violent, and would often beat him. His tough grandfather took him in and taught him to work hard. But unfortunately, his grandfather communicated much negativity towards him: "You will never amount to anything, *never*! You will grow up and be no good, just like your old man, Roberson."

At sixteen, Dave got saved in a Pentecostal church, but no one followed up to mentor him. He backslid after two weeks. He joined the Navy for a term, and then after his discharge, he returned to God in an extremely legalistic Holiness church, and that is where he found his wife, Rosalie. He got baptized in the Holy Spirit there and from that point on, he had no problem staying faithful to God. Dave worked at a lumber mill and would often share the gospel with all the men around him.

At thirty years old, Dave woke up one morning feeling a strong sense of the presence of God. He opened his eyes, and instead of seeing the walls of his bedroom, he saw an auditorium with people in wheelchairs waiting on the platform. He was seated three rows back on the left side. Somehow, he knew that this meeting was supposed to be *his* meeting. The associate pastor began to announce the speaker, and he looked right at Dave. Dave had his Bible open to the book of Jude, verses 20-21, which teach about praying in tongues. Dave started to stand up, but suddenly, the associate pointed to the stage curtain, and out came a blond woman who moved mightily in the power and anointing of the Holy Spirit. All the people in the wheelchairs were healed. Then suddenly, the auditorium became empty except for Dave and the woman preacher. She looked at him and said: "I don't know why God has given me this kind of ministry; one of you men must have failed."

Dave was shaking when he came back out of the vision. He asked his wife if she would support his call to the ministry no matter what, and she said she would. Two weeks later, he quit his job.

He decided to start praying. In an old bowling alley where they were holding Christian services, there was a side room where he began to dedicate time in prayer. He thought that if he prayed with the schedule he'd had at the lumber mill, then God would provide for his needs just like the company had paid him for his work. He prayed in English but ran out of things to pray for in just fifteen minutes. So, he started praying in tongues. Whenever the whistle at the lumber mill would blow for break time, Dave would take a break and get some coffee at a nearby coffee shop. But he would return to his position in his prayer room at the bowling alley when the break at the lumber mill was over. He would pray until the lunch whistle at the mill blew.

Then, after lunch, he would pray in tongues until dinner time. The hours went by slowly. They seemed to take forever. But he kept on going doing what he had determined to do, and for three long months he kept to his schedule.

Then, after three months of praying in tongues eight hours a day, he was invited to attend a service in another church taking place one afternoon. Very happy to get out of his prayer closet, he went. But it was a disappointment. The speaker was spiritually dead, very dry, and boring. Dave stirred his coffee and turned to look at the older lady sitting next to him. When he did, to his amazement, he saw what looked like an x-ray picture of the woman's hip. He realized that she needed healing, and that God would heal her! He told the older lady, "Ma'am, you are having trouble with your hip." Then, the word arthritis came to his mind. "You have arthritis in your hip!" She affirmed it. He prayed for her, and she was healed! This started some excitement in the church service, where another woman got healed and the young people in the church got baptized in the Holy Spirit.

Later, God spoke to Dave and told him that what happened at the other church was for no other reason than to teach him a spiritual principle—he had learned to build himself up spiritually by praying in tongues. Dave would also learn to combine prayer in tongues with fasting, even doing a forty-day fast. Dave Roberson went on to plant a large church and to minister in healing power for forty-nine more years. In 2022, he passed away at seventy-nine years of age.[15]

Prayer Beats Pride

In the previous chapter, I highlighted that when prayer, fasting, and giving are combined, they help defeat our three primary temptations of pride, lust, and greed. Prayerlessness is a form of pride. Life without prayer is like boasting against God that you are independent and don't need Him. I would say that the real reason people don't pray is not because they are too busy, but because they are proud, dependent only upon themselves. If you say you don't have time for prayer, stop blaming your busy schedule; instead, repent of your pride. You will always find time to do what you really want to do!

Pride is idolatrous worship of self. It's the national religion of hell. That's what made a certain angel of God become the devil. The prophet Jeremiah declared God's curse on those who placed their trust in themselves instead of in Him.

> *Cursed is the man who trusts in man, who depends on flesh for his strength, whose heart turns away from the Lord. He will be like a bush in the wastelands.*
> (Jeremiah 17:5)

They will become like a dry bush in the desert, a tumbleweed. No root, no greenery, no fruit. Busy but not fruitful. A lot of activity but no productivity. Life that is not birthed out of prayer is like running on a treadmill, sweating but going nowhere. It's impossible to burn for God without putting in this prayer log. Prayer is firewood that we must bring to the altar to keep our fire burning.

The enemy attacks prayer because prayer attacks the enemy. He knows that he can't stop God from answering our prayers, so he fights hard to keep us from praying to God. When the king made a decree in Daniel's day to stop his daily prayer life, Daniel did not budge. He continued to pray three times a day as had been his determined custom (Daniel 6:10). Daniel would rather spend a night with lions than spend a day without prayer. Think about that!

Sin leads to prayerlessness, and prayerlessness leads to more sin. Being prayerless is a sin. Samuel said it best:

> *Moreover, as for me, far be it from me that I should sin against the LORD in ceasing to pray for you; but I will teach you the good and the right way.*
> (1 Samuel 12:23)

Someone once said, "A praying man will stop sinning, and a sinning man will stop praying." How true is that? What did Adam do when he sinned? He hid from God. He ran from the Lord. Sin causes us to hide from God; prayer helps us to hide in God. One day God came to Adam and asked, "Where are you?" God is still asking that question to all of us. Where are you? Why are you not in prayer? If you have sinned, run to God for cleansing; don't wallow in sin and guilt.

When Your Prayer Life Goes to Sleep

The flesh attacks prayer, and prayer attacks the flesh. The flesh doesn't want us to pray. Like the disciples in the garden of Gethsemane, many of us yield to the demands of the flesh and sleep instead of praying. We lose the battle with a pillow and blankets. Sooner or later, sleeping saints become slipping saints. These words of Jesus challenge me every time, "What! Could you not watch with Me for one hour? Watch and pray, lest you enter into temptation. The spirit indeed is willing, but the flesh is weak" (Matthew 26:40-41). Do you love Jesus enough to join Him in prayer?

Victory in prayer brings victory in life. Lack of prayer brings defeat in many other areas. Prayer builds up the spirit of a man; prayerlessness only strengthens the flesh. Pray when you do feel like praying and pray even when you don't feel like praying! It's a sin to neglect opportunities to pray together with Jesus. Not praying is spiritual negligence and it's dangerous to remain in that condition.

I find it interesting that Peter slept instead of praying with Jesus, and as a result he received a warning. "And the Lord said, 'Simon, Simon! Indeed, Satan has asked for you, that he may sift you as wheat. But I have prayed for you, that your faith should not fail; and when you have returned to Me, strengthen your brethren'" (Luke 22:31-32). Previously, Jesus had changed Simon's name to Peter which means "a solid rock."[16] From then on, Jesus called Peter by his new name, but this time in the garden of Gethsemane, when Peter was caught sleeping instead of praying, Jesus called him by his old name twice. Could it be that when our prayer life goes to sleep, our past life wakes up? If we don't pray, we stray. If we don't watch and pray, we end up with temptations which so often overcome us. Our old life is dead, but the lack of prayer can resurrect it. That is how much detrimental power there is in a prayerless life.

One time when Satan asked for Peter, Jesus prayed for him, but Peter himself didn't bother to pray. It makes sense why he ended up denying his best friend—his overconfidence led him to prayerlessness, which resulted in him denying Christ three times. Jesus wrestled in prayer, which gave Him power to resist temptation, but Peter slept in prayer, which resulted in no power to resist temptation.

Not only does the flesh get the upper hand when we don't pray, but spiritual battles in the unseen realm will turn in the enemy's favor. When Jesus prayed in the garden, God sent an angel to support Him. When Paul prayed in the storm, God sent His angel to assist them. When the church prayed for Peter, God sent an angel to deliver him. Jentezen Franklin once said, "Prayerlessness is the unemployment of angels." When you don't pray, God doesn't answer! When you don't pray, God's angels are unemployed. You will fight a spiritual battle alone and you will most likely lose.

Prayer is Not Pointless

We need to understand that prayer is not all about getting what we want from God. Prayer does indeed bring us results, but more than anything, it brings a reward. Jesus said,

> *But you, when you pray, go into your room, and when you have shut your door, pray to your Father who is in the secret place; and your Father who sees in secret will reward you openly.*
>
> (Matthew 6:6)

His presence is our reward. When Abraham asked God for a son, God gave him encouraging assurance way before He answered with a miracle.

> *After these things the word of the LORD came to Abram in a vision, saying, "Do not be afraid, Abram. I am your shield, your exceedingly great reward."*
>
> (Genesis 15:1)

Many people are disappointed in prayer because they don't get answers when they want or the way they expect. Prayer is much more than getting results; it's about getting the awesome, warm presence of God in your heart.

Unanswered prayers can become a discouraging hindrance to a person's prayer life. As a teenager, I prayed earnestly for God to heal my eye. There was nothing wrong with my vision, but the eyelid was weaker in the left eye, and the eye itself wouldn't go up whenever I looked up. Factory defect–it came from my birth. That affected my self-esteem, which resulted in some bullying and name-calling at school. The enemy would put lies into my head: *Why pray? Why fast? Why seek God when He doesn't even care about you?* But those were lies targeting my connection to my loving Father. I made promises to God that if He would heal me, then I would always live for Him and testify of His miracle power. To this very day, that prayer hasn't been answered. Even though I stopped praying that specific prayer a long time ago, I do believe that someday in heaven, I will have perfect eyes. And while here on earth, this issue doesn't stop me from being who God called me to be or from doing what He wants me to do. I refuse to let the devil mess up my prayer life just because of my physical defect. Remember, God didn't answer Jesus' prayer when He was in the garden pleading for God to remove the cup of suffering from Him. Yet, Jesus continued to pray—in the garden, on the cross, and after His resurrection. In fact, Jesus continues to make daily intercession for us (Romans 8:34).

There is a story about a man named Ivan, who endured the horrors of a Soviet prison camp. One day he was praying with his eyes closed when a fellow prisoner noticed him and said with ridicule, "Prayers won't help you get out of here any faster." Opening his eyes, Ivan answered, "I do not pray to get out of prison but to do the will of God."[17] Prayer is not only about the results; it's also about seeking to do God's will. We can't move

God; prayer is to move us. There are many instances in the Bible of prayer bringing results. The Bible records 650 prayers and 450 answers to prayers. The Bible also tells us that we need to wait upon the Lord so that He can renew our strength (Isaiah 40:31). Of course I want prayer to remove my problems, but so often in prayer, the Lord renews my strength and deepens my relationship with Him, which is my *great reward.*

Some may ask, *If God does what He wants to do regardless of whether I pray, what's the point of praying?* Well, God is faithful to His promises, and one of His promises is to answer prayers. Moreover, He loves to answer His people's prayers. Israel cried out for the exodus from slavery in Egypt, something God had promised Abraham 430 years earlier (Genesis 15:13, Exodus 12:40). In due time, God sent Moses as an answer to their desperate cries in prayer, not just to fulfill His promise, but to answer their pleas (Exodus 3:7-10). God promised Elijah to send rain upon the land, yet Elijah had to pray earnestly seven times for the rain to start; the rain came as an answer to his prayers, not just as a fulfillment of God's promise (1 Kings 18:41-45). Daniel prayed for the release of his people from captivity in Babylon, something Jeremiah had prophesied seventy years earlier (Daniel 9:2-3, Jeremiah 29:10). God promised the Holy Spirit for the disciples, but Jesus still prayed over His followers to receive the promise of the Father (Acts 1:4-5, John 14:16-17). God will fulfill His promise, but He delights to hear your prayers and answer them. Maybe that's why Paul told Timothy to wage war in accordance with the prophecies given to him (1 Timothy 1:18; 4:14). Don't fall into this trap of assuming that if God wants to do something, He will do it whether you pray or not. He wants you to demonstrate your dependence on Him by asking, praying, and seeking.

Jesus Prayed and So Should You

Jesus was fully God and fully human. Though He was God and had a unique relationship with His Father, He also lived on our level here on earth. When He took on the limitations of a physical body, He showed us that a life of prayer is a necessity, not a luxury! Jesus lived in complete dependence on the Father, and so should we.

Jesus prayed on earth, He prayed in heaven, and He continues to intercede for us always. Jesus' current job is intercession. Let that sink in. He lives to make intercession for us. "Therefore He is also able to save to the uttermost those who come to God through Him, since He always lives to make intercession for them" (Hebrews 7:25). If prayer doesn't matter, why did Jesus do it when He was on earth? Why does He bother to intercede for us in heaven? Why does God invite us to ask in order to receive answers to what He's already promised in the Bible? If prayer doesn't make any difference, it's only a pointless babble of words into empty space.

If we really want to know how to live burning for God, Jesus is our role model. He prayed while being baptized by John the Baptist in the river. When I got baptized, I focused more on not getting water into my nose; but Jesus prayed. "…And while He prayed, the heaven was opened" (Luke 3:21). While He prayed, the heavens were opened. While He prayed, the Holy Spirit descended. While He prayed, a voice came from heaven. While He prayed…. We don't know what He asked for, but we do know that heaven responded to His prayer. Prayer opens the heavens. Prayer brings about the Holy Spirit's manifest presence. God said to Him, "You are My beloved Son, in whom I am well pleased" (Mark 1:11). Prayer helps us to hear God's voice more clearly. Prayer brings God's approval.

There is another instance when Jesus went up on a mountain and prayed. "As He prayed, the appearance of His face was altered, and His robe became white and glistening" (Luke 9:29). As He prayed, His face was changed. As He prayed, His robe became white. As He prayed, Moses and Elijah showed up. Again, we don't know the content of that prayer, but we do see its effects. Faith changes things, but prayer changes us. Prayer causes personal transformation. Our faces will change. Our attitude will change. Prayer changes the spiritual atmosphere around us. God's peace will replace stress. God's joy will replace sadness. Light will expel darkness.

Jesus prayed before making important decisions. Early in His ministry, Jesus spent the whole night alone in prayer; then, the next day He chose His twelve disciples. Luke records: "So He Himself often withdrew into the wilderness and prayed" (Luke 5:16). Many times, after long days of ministry, Jesus would withdraw to be alone and pray.

Jesus prayed to work through grief. After Jesus learned that His cousin John the Baptist had been beheaded, He went away by Himself to a deserted place. After His time there, He resumed His ministry to the multitudes who had followed Him to that place. Yes, even the Son of God grieves. He grieved in prayer. As I mentioned earlier, Jesus prayed in times of distress. Hours before He was arrested, He went to the Mt. of Olives to pray and kneeled a short distance away from His disciples. He was in great emotional agony, knowing what He was about to face. Jesus prayed.

No wonder His disciples asked Him to teach them to pray. They saw the source of His power. When the early apostles' ministry exploded after Jesus' departure and they got very busy serving people, they realized they needed to return to the ministry of the word and prayer (Acts 6:1-4). Busyness wasn't an excuse for Jesus to skip prayer. At times, He was super busy in His ministry, but He always took time to pray. Francis de Sales said, "Every Christian needs a half-hour of prayer each day, except when he is busy; then he needs an hour."

I want to refer to the vision I described in an earlier chapter when God showed me a picture of my future in the grocery store parking lot. One thing that caught my attention there was that at the back of the store, there were big double doors where semi-trucks would deliver produce. I immediately sensed the Lord telling me that the Church should have the front door open to evangelism, discipleship, small groups, media ministry, kids' ministry, and youth ministry, but the back door of the church needs to be open too. The back door is the door where God's angels and the Holy Spirit can bring spiritual "produce"–this door is prayer and fasting. If the church is not a house of prayer, it will become a den of thieves. If it is a house of prayer, God will bring His resources to it. That's why our church, Hungry Generation, has doors open at 5:00 a.m. Monday through Friday for prayer. If Jesus always prayed, why do we think we can ignore prayer?

Prayer is one of the logs that keeps the fire on your altar burning. Pride, not busyness, is what keeps us from prayer. The Bible has nothing good to say about pride. Pride is an excessive focus on self, resulting in arrogance and conceit. It's like an egocentric self-idolatry which puts God and others in second and last place.

> In his pride the wicked does not seek him [God]; in
> all his thoughts there is no room for God.
> (Psalm 10:4 NIV)

Prayer defeats pride because by praying we declare our total dependence on God.

The fire on our altar will keep burning if we keep adding logs of prayer to it. If you want to learn more about prayer and how to pray, check out Appendix 3 at the end of the book.

CHAPTER 10

The Stick of Fasting

I n our church at the beginning of each new year, we join millions of believers worldwide for a twenty-one-day fast. In January of 2023, I was in Romania where I preached at the OneThing conference. It was my first time in Romania and the Lord did wonderful things at that conference. I returned from the conference overflowing with joy but was also extremely sick. It wasn't just a normal fever; I thought I was dying. I ended up going to the emergency room to see a doctor. And at the same time, we were just beginning a twenty-one-day fast at our church. I had invited our church and all the online viewers to join us for that period of fasting, and I promised that I would be streaming words of encouragement over the internet to them every day during the twenty-one days. So, I was wondering, *Should I cancel the fast for me personally and not stream, or should I do the fast while sick and still stream?* I asked the doctor about it, and he said that fasting would help me to recover faster, not slow down my healing. You can still see in videos during the first day of fasting in 2023 how my lips were all swollen. I was really sick that day, but by the third day, my fever broke, and by God's grace, I was able to finish the 21-day fast and get the breakthrough I needed.

I learned an important truth about having a fever while fasting. See, I always thought that a fever was a bad thing and that I should get rid of it, but the doctor told me that a fever could be good. It is a temporary increase in body temperature in response to a disease or illness. When your body has an infection, your immune system kicks into gear to help you heal. One way it does this is by increasing your body temperature, which we call a *fever*. The higher temperature helps your body fight off infections more effectively by making it harder for the germs to survive and multiply.

Fasting has the same effect as a fever. It increases the spiritual temperature in which spiritual germs can't survive. John Wesley, leader of a great revival movement, once said, "When you seek God with fasting, added to prayer, you cannot seek His face in vain." Whenever Charles Grandison Finney, leader of the Second Great Awakening, detected any weakness in his life, he would change his schedule, set aside one or several days, and fast. Fasting increases the spiritual heat in your life. Jonathan Edwards, who led the Frontier Revivals, is said to have fasted and prayed until he was so weak that he could hardly stand in the pulpit. And God amazingly anointed his ministry. Andrew Murray, missionary statesman and church leader, once said, "Fasting helps to express, to deepen and confirm the resolution that we are ready to sacrifice anything, to sacrifice ourselves to attain what we seek for the kingdom of God."

Every noteworthy person mentioned in the Bible practiced fasting: Moses, David, Elijah, Esther, Daniel, Anna, and Paul, just to name a few. Our Lord Jesus practiced fasting. In fact, He began His itinerant ministry after a forty-day period of fasting. When He taught on the subject of fasting, He said, *"When* you fast" not *"If* you fast" (Matthew 6:16-17) His critics noticed that His disciples did not fast like John's disciples did, but Jesus told them that they would fast after He left the earth (Matthew 9:14-15). He assumed that all His followers would fast, and His disciples did just that. The early church fasted every Wednesday and Friday. In those days, fasting was a normal preparation for water baptism and communion. The believers would fast to strengthen their prayer life, prepare for God's revelation, express sorrow, help the poor with the food they saved while fasting, and reconnect with God.

We human beings were created to fast. Think about it: if you sleep eight hours a day, then you are sleeping away one-third of your life. If you live to seventy-five years, that's twenty-five years of sleeping, or 9,125 days. When you are asleep, you are fasting and that's why the morning meal is called "break-fast." When you eat breakfast, you break your fast. Biblical fasting is abstaining from food for spiritual reasons. It's voluntary, not forced. Sometimes circumstances force starvation but fasting is a decision you make. You choose to let go of the enchantment of food for a certain period of time in order to seek God. It's not a diet or a hunger strike. During fasting, we feed ourselves with God's Word.

Except by Prayer and Fasting

While Jesus was on a high mountain praying with three of His disciples, the other disciples were at the foot of the mountain dealing with a distressing problem they couldn't resolve. Surrounded by a crowd of spectators, they tried but failed to deliver a boy of evil spirits. When Jesus came down from the mountaintop, he found that some religious leaders were disputing with His disciples. The father of the tormented child begged Jesus for help. But instead of immediately healing the boy, Jesus replied with some very harsh words to the crowd: "O faithless and perverse generation, how long shall I be with you? How long shall I bear with you? Bring him here to Me" (Matthew 17:17).

The generation from two thousand years ago was faithless and perverse, but our generation is the same—a generation without faith and with many perversions. Faith deals with our connection to God and perversion deals with our connection to this world. Our generation today is not connected to God, but it is connected to this wicked, broken, and sinful world. Jesus was tired of it. And He still is. The less connected we are to the Lord, the more connected we are to this world; and the more connected we are to the world, the less connected we are to the Lord.

Jesus kindly healed the boy. The disciples later asked Him why they couldn't get the same results. Jesus pointed out that it was not a lack of authority, and definitely not because it wasn't God's will for them to heal the boy, but because of their unbelief (Matthew 17:20). Then He added, "However, this kind does not go out except by prayer and fasting" (Matthew 17:21). This statement is repeated in Mark 9:29. Certain things get broken only when we pray and fast.

As a little side note, this verse is actually omitted in some translations of the Bible, especially in the paraphrased Bibles. Most of the oldest, original Greek manuscripts do not include this verse, which some translators view as the most reliable manuscripts to use. However, the majority of manuscripts written in Greek do have this verse mentioning prayer and fasting. Matthew wrote primarily to the Jewish people and included fasting in Matthew 17:21, a practice which was already quite common to them.

If the problem with this generation is faithlessness and perversion, then Jesus' solution is prayer and fasting. If faithlessness disconnects you from God, and perversion connects you to the world, then prayer connects you to God, and fasting disconnects you from the world.

Fasting disconnects you from something that powerfully connects you to this world: food. Through prayer, we relink with the Lord, and with fasting, we detach from this tangible physical realm. Prayer and fasting are the characteristics of mountaintop people. They are connected to God and disconnected from the world. Mountaintop people can handle valley-type problems. This generation is wicked, God is raising up for Himself a generation of wild ones. It's a radical thing to pray and fast, but that's what it takes to combat problems in the world around us.

Jesus came down from the mountain of prayer where He had been fasting. I don't believe there were any fast-food restaurants there on the mountain where He spent the day with three disciples. When He came down, He confronted the demonic and demonstrated that spiritual problems are not won with natural weapons. As they say, you don't bring a knife to a gunfight. A lack of close connection to God and much connection to the world leaves anyone unprepared to face and win spiritual battles.

Here's an interesting fact about eagles: They don't fight snakes on the ground. Because snakes cannot strike unless they are coiled on the ground, an eagle will pick up a snake, fly high into the sky, and change the snake's battleground. Then the eagle will release the snake into the air, where it is useless, weak, and vulnerable. On the ground, snakes are powerful, wise, and deadly; in the air, they are helpless.

The Scripture mentions eagles when it encourages believers to trust/wait upon the Lord. Like an eagle, don't fight the enemy in his own territory—come up higher. Learn to take your fight from the ground into the spiritual realm by praying and fasting. Prayer and fasting are mighty weapons of warfare in the spiritual realm! When you connect to God and disconnect from this world, God takes over your battles and enables you to win. When you pray and fast, you are taking your personal battles into the spiritual realm, where Satan is useless, helpless, and without authority. A lack of prayer and fasting causes you to fight spiritual battles with only physical means. The snake wins. The devil is a deceiving expert in the realm of the flesh and the world.

Defeating King Stomach

I love good food—especially Russian food. Food is not evil or demonic. There are many verses in the Bible about food; it is presented as a good thing, and enjoying food is a gift of God (Proverbs 13:25; Ecclesiastes 3:13). Consumption of food is necessary for survival (Nehemiah 5:1-2; Acts 27:33-35). Eating is a sign of life and health (Deuteronomy 28:4-11). God blesses His people with sufficient food (Psalm 34:8-10).

With that said, do not forget that Adam and Eve ate themselves out of the Garden because the tree was pleasant to the eyes and good for food (Genesis 3:6). Esau sold his birthright for the bowl of soup because he was famished with hunger and thought he would die (Genesis 25:31-34). God judged the people of Sodom for their pride, fullness of food, abundance of idleness, and abominations (Ezra 16:49). Israel yielded to an intense craving for meat, which resulted in a plague (Numbers 11:4, 33-34). Our Savior, Jesus', first temptation in the wilderness was with food (Luke 4:3). Is food sinful? Absolutely not. But gluttony is. Gluttony is defined as the overindulgence or lack of self-restraint with food and drink. The dictionary defines gluttony as "excess in eating or drinking, greedy or excessive indulgence." Gluttony induces laziness and results in hopelessness (Titus 1:12; 1 Corinthians 15:32). It brings poverty (Proverbs 23:21). Gluttony is associated with rebellion, stubbornness, and wastefulness (Deuteronomy 21:20). In 1 Samuel 2:12-17, 34, the high priest Eli had two disobedient sons who were also priests before the Lord and were greedy for the best cuts of the sacrificial animals. God punished them with death. They were corrupt, wayward, defiant, and practiced adultery with women who came to the Tabernacle (1 Samuel 2:22-24). Even Eli was excessively fat and died of a broken neck when he fell backward off his seat.

Gluttony is making a god out of your belly. It's called idolatry when food becomes an idol, something you focus on obsessively. Gluttony impels one to eat excessively at all hours of the day or night. It messes with a person's mind, making him think that he needs to eat more and to snack all the time. That's called unrestrained binge eating. Jesus taught us by His straightforward response to the devil in the wilderness that eating should not be one's chief priority (Matthew 4:1-4). Man shall not live by bread alone!

The apostle Paul warned of the stomach becoming a god: "Whose end is destruction, whose god is their belly, and whose glory is in their shame—who set their mind on earthly things" (Philippians 3:19). When the desires of your body become the master of your life, your stomach can easily become a god of overconsumption, eating more than is necessary. What Paul described in Philippians 3:19 is the result of letting your stomach run wild; and this doesn't even begin to mention the serious health issues that overeating brings.

I don't mean any personal insult to those who really are struggling with their weight caused by reasons other than unhealthy life choices. Many believers today criticize the sins of lust and pride in others but haven't addressed the sin of gluttony in their own lives. We are not called to live carnal lives but crucified ones. "And those who are Christ's have crucified the flesh with its passions and desires" (Galatians 5:24).

Fasting is a great way to subdue the appetites of the flesh. It's not the only way, but it's a very effective way. Fasting is preparation for freedom from bondage to your flesh. When you're fasting, you're training your body that it doesn't get what it wants. Your body is no longer your master—the Lord is. The stomach is no longer in control—the Holy Spirit is.

Affliction of the Soul

Israel was commanded to fast once a year on the Day of Atonement. The command for this fast was, "You shall afflict your souls" (Leviticus 16:31). Thus, fasting is an affliction of the soul. I find it interesting that it doesn't say it afflicts your body. Sometimes it does seem like a physical affliction. But here, we see fasting as a suffering of the soul (the seat of your mind, will, and emotions). David mentioned a similar thing: "When I wept and chastened my soul with fasting, That became my reproach" (Psalm 69:10). Also, God rebuked the Israelites for the wrong fast they practiced in Isaiah 58:3: "'Why have we fasted,' they say, 'and You have not seen? Why have we afflicted our souls, and You take no notice?'" There is a connection between fasting and the affliction of the soul. Fasting is not only physical, but also emotional and mental. It takes willpower. Fasting exposes how much influence your soul has over your life. That is why when you fast, your soul will throw a fit. You might feel cranky and irritable, useless, doubtful, mentally attacked, or second guess yourself, but that's totally normal—it's an affliction of the soul.

Fasting openly exposes the unhealthy relationship we have with food. Food is not your friend! It is meant only to nourish your body's cells. Whenever good food makes people feel happy, they often satisfy their negative emotions or boredom with eating. They call it comfort food when excess food becomes a comfort to you. God has promised the Holy Spirit to be our Comforter. The enemy wants us to turn to the fridge for comfort. When you fast, you are forced to deal with these toxic emotions in a new way by bringing them to the Holy Spirit instead of finding false comfort in food. Fasting from eating food trains us to share our feelings with the Father instead of with the fridge or the pantry. That process of sanctification is a good affliction for the soul.

Fasting helps to move us from being soulish Christians to being spiritual Christians by putting the soul where it belongs: in the back seat. Many believers let their soul control their life instead of their spirit, but fasting helps to break the dominion of the soul. We have a soul, but we don't have to be manipulated by our soul. We should be spiritual, not carnal. If we live in our soul, it's time to turn around and start living controlled by the Holy Spirit. Sometimes, we have to do what David did. He spoke to his soul. "Why are you cast down, O my soul? And why are you disquieted within me? Hope in God, for I shall yet praise Him. For the help of His countenance" (Psalm 42:5). Be firm and speak to your soul.

During your fast, not only will physical toxins be removed, but emotional toxins will go as well. Allow the Holy Spirit to cleanse you of soul toxins during the fast. Fasting afflicts, humbles, and weakens the soul's control. You don't need to fast for your spirit, since it's already sealed by the Holy Spirit and made perfect by Jesus' sacrifice. Our spirit is not the problem; it's the soul that is a hindrance. Fasting helps to break that soulish barrier in the spirit realm so we can live more spiritual lives.

Detoxing Your Body

Although there are many spiritual benefits to fasting, there are also a variety of practical health benefits that come from abstaining from food. Benjamin Franklin said, "The best of all medicine is rest and fasting," and Mark Twain said, "It's said a little starvation can really do more for the average sick person than the best medicine and the best doctors." Although these comments are not from medical professionals, there is some wisdom in their words. I noticed even my dog stops eating when he is sick. We humans do the same: when we are sick, we lose our appetite, our body goes into full-blown assault, and all hands are on deck to fight the virus or sickness. It's not a time to feed; it's a time to fight.

When you fast, your body switches from burning glucose to burning ketones. Glucose is a type of sugar that comes from the carbohydrates you like, such as bread, pasta, fruits, and vegetables. When these foods are digested, they are broken down into glucose. Glucose goes into the bloodstream and your cells use it as their primary energy source. The second energy source that your body begins to rely on when you're abstaining from food during fasting is ketones. Ketones are produced by your liver when your body doesn't have enough glucose for energy. When your body runs low on glucose, it breaks down stored fat into ketones. These ketones become an alternative energy source for you. Think of ketones as your body's backup energy source. In other words, when you're fasting, your body has a backup source of energy for your muscles, brain, and other organs. When you fast, you go into ketosis, and your body turns to those stores of fat for the energy it needs. As it gets rid of that extra fat, it also has some detoxifying effects on the body.[18]

Something interesting takes place physically during fasting. It's called autophagy. Autophagy is like a recycling and cleaning process inside your body's cells. It's an ongoing cellular process that is augmented by fasting for even one or two days. Imagine your cells cluttered with a lot of old, broken parts (like old rusty machinery) and waste. Autophagy is the process that breaks down all this unwanted stuff in the cells and recycles it into new, useful parts. It helps keep your cells healthy and efficient by eliminating what they don't need. When you fast and don't eat for a certain period, this process of autophagy speeds up. Normally, your cells use the food you eat as energy. But when you're fasting, your cells don't get this regular food energy supply. As a result, they start a deep cleaning process, breaking down the old parts and waste to create energy. Think of it this way: If you didn't have wood and you were freezing and hungry, you would burn whatever you could find. You'd even start using old furniture as firewood to keep warm and cook food. This deep cleaning during fasting helps your cells stay healthy and even helps prevent some diseases.

In a breakthrough described as "remarkable," scientists have found that fasting for as little as three days can regenerate the entire immune system, even for the elderly. Although fasting diets have been criticized by nutritionists as being unhealthy, new research suggests that starving the body kickstarts stem cells into producing new white blood cells, which fight off infection. In a 2003 mouse study overseen by Mark Mattson, head of the National Institute on Aging's neuroscience laboratory, mice that fasted regularly were healthier by some measures than the mice subjected to continuous calorie restriction; they had lower levels of insulin and glucose in their blood, for example, which signified increased sensitivity to insulin and a reduced risk of diabetes.[19]

Fasting is also great for the liver. When your body isn't being bombarded with salts, colorants, sugars, and artificial chemicals, it gets a chance to rest—and your body gets a chance to process and get rid of all the harmful accumulated chemicals. Fasting puts your body through a rejuvenating experience. It dissolves diseased cells, leaving only healthy tissue. There's also a noticeable redistribution of nutrients in the body. The body hangs onto precious vitamins and minerals while processing and removing old tissue, toxins, or undesirable materials.[20] There are also incredible cleansing and heart health benefits that take place during a fast. As your basal metabolic rate (BMR—the rate at which your body burns calories) lowers, fat in the blood starts to disappear because it's metabolized for energy. This process promotes a healthy heart, and for some, improves cholesterol levels by boosting HDL (high-density lipoprotein) levels.[21]

Fasting promotes blood sugar control by reducing insulin resistance, which can be helpful in maintaining good blood sugar levels.[22] It also helps with fighting inflammation in the body.[23] Fasting does aid weight loss, which we all know for sure, and it boosts metabolism.[24] Fasting could delay aging and extend longevity. Studies on this are currently limited to animals. However, in one study, rats that fasted every other day experienced a delayed rate of aging and lived 83% longer than rats that didn't fast.[25]

Do you want a healthier body? Practice fasting. Want to get closer to God? Practice fasting. Want to maintain a healthy spiritual life? Practice both fasting and prayer. Fasting rids one's soul of accumulated toxic wastes of the world and the flesh, and it gives a person a renewed desire to walk alongside God in holiness. Add fasting to your bundle of sticks to make your fire burn even hotter.

Fasting will enhance your ability to cast out demons and gain renewed authority over every evil spirit in the spirit realm around you. Come to Jesus for a cleansing through fasting and prayer. In the next chapter, we're going to see how sacrificial, generous giving will cleanse your soul of greed and pride.

CHAPTER 11

The Stick of Sacrifice

chicken and a pig were walking down the lane and saw a poor farmer. The chicken said to the pig, "Let's make him breakfast. I will give him an egg and you give him some bacon." The pig replied, "Giving an egg is easy for you; but for me, to give him bacon is a sacrifice." A chicken can easily give an egg as an offering, but for a pig, giving bacon will cost him his life. I can say that for most of my Christian life, I was the chicken who gave God what didn't cost me—that which didn't hurt my wallet. From my teenage years, my dad taught us the principle of tithing—giving ten percent of our income to God. But I never grew beyond that. As a Christian, I was a tightwad. I heard people talk about sowing and giving sacrificially, but in my mind, they were wackos and manipulators. And some of them really were just that.

But my world changed when it came to making a certain sacrifice in 2013. I had been married a few years already and had been the youth pastor for more than a decade, but I was not seeing the revival I believed God had promised us. We were stuck in a rut and spiritually stagnant. It was as though there was an invisible ceiling over our ministry where we couldn't go any higher to fulfill God's calling.

One day I was on my way to preach at a youth conference in California. On the Alaska Airlines flight, I was sitting on an aisle seat, listening to a sermon by a pastor from another country. This pastor shared his personal testimony of how God brought revival in his ministry through making a financial sacrifice. His ministry was at a standstill with no results. So, when he received a $10,000 inheritance, he decided to sow it into God's kingdom, hoping for a revival. I remember listening to this and thinking, *That's stupid. You can't buy revival. God doesn't need our money.* However, the reason I was listening to this minister was because there was abundant fruit in his ministry which I wanted in ours: people being saved, churches being planted, demons cast out, and notable healings taking place.

I felt a still, small voice telling me to sow an offering the way this man had. At first, I rejected that thought, and in my foolishness, I rebuked the devil. There was no way God would ask me to give away my hard-earned savings. My wife and I were living from month to month on our earnings, trying to save up money. Interestingly, in the first few years of our marriage, with much diligence and scrimping, we had saved $10,000 at the time I was listening to this pastor's message. In our bank account, we had the same amount he had given away. Well, I went to this youth conference to preach, and every time I stopped to pray, I heard this prompting, "Empty your bank account and give all your savings to a ministry that is producing fruit." I was confused. Was this God, me, or the devil? So, I did the basic math in my head. This couldn't be me because I am not that generous. I was actually pretty stingy. I don't think this was the devil because he doesn't represent generosity, especially in supporting God's kingdom work. Maybe this was manipulation from the preacher I listened to on the podcast. But the preacher didn't actually tell people to do the same thing he'd done. I was left with the painful truth: This could be the Lord. I decided to put it out of my head and I told the Lord, "If this is really from You, if when I let my wife know about this idea and she responds without much hesitation, then I'll know for sure it's You!" I knew she wouldn't allow me to give away our hard-earned savings because we had plans to buy land and build a house.

That thought, impression, and the idea of giving away all our savings didn't leave me after returning home from the youth conference. It took me three days to work up the courage to even present this idea to my wife. Then, I told her that maybe God is telling us to take all our savings and give it away in order to position ourselves for a spiritual breakthrough. I thought she would jump up and call me crazy. But she responded with something that made things even more difficult for me. She replied, "If you feel that this is Lord's leading, I'm in agreement with you. Let's do it." I thought, *What did I get myself into? Now my wife thinks I'm some kind of prophet, but I'm not even sure if it's the Lord's perfect will.* To cut the story short, we decided to give that money away to a ministry that was producing fruit. It was December 2013, and we received a letter from that ministry with a dedicated prayer. It was a short prayer that revival would begin taking place in our youth group. I felt really good like as though something was going to change.

But nothing changed. The church remained the same. I started to give a call for salvation every service, but no one was responding. We didn't even have lost people in the church. I decided to pray for healing in almost every service, but I didn't hear of anyone getting healed from those prayers. It was pretty disappointing.

The new year (2014) rolled in, and the ministry into which we sowed $10,000 called us and said that they were praying for us. I was overjoyed. Then one of the intercessors on the line said, "God told us something about your ministry." I couldn't wait to hear what God said. We got connected on Skype and she said, "God told us to tell you to start giving $1,000 a month into our ministry." My reaction was the same as yours right now! *What? Are you crazy? That's manipulation. I won't do this.* I hung up the Skype call and removed them from my Skype account so they couldn't contact me again. I thought, *I gave my savings in response to God's leading, not because someone told me I had to. Now they think they can get more. Plus, I can't save more than a few hundred dollars each month.*

The next morning, I felt the impression from the Holy Spirit to trust God for the next twelve months and give $1,000 to that ministry. My wife and I surrendered and told God that if He provided that amount of money, we would give it. If we didn't have it, we wouldn't give it. We agreed to test Him for a year, not because someone on Skype told us to, but because we felt this was actually from the Lord. For the next four months, we didn't notice anything different happening in the church. We ourselves started to experience financial setbacks. We lost tenants in our only rental property and couldn't find any others for four long months. I had never encountered anything like this in my life; my mind was freaking out.

But then I began to experience God's intervention, which started with someone messaging me on Facebook asking for my address so they could send me a check. I had a few hundred followers on Facebook, but nobody really knew who I was. Then a letter arrived and when I opened the envelope, I found a check for exactly $1,000. God provided the seed I was supposed to give. Then I traveled to another youth conference where they gave me an honorarium, which was enough for the next three months' seed. I encountered Jehovah Jireh, the God who provides.

It's interesting how when God revealed Himself as Jehovah Jireh to Abraham, He provided a sacrifice for him. We learn about God's name Jehovah Jireh in Genesis 22:13-14. God didn't provide for Abraham's needs or bills, but for a sacrifice that God Himself requested from him. I always thought that my provider God provides only for my needs, but in those few months, I met the God who also provides a seed.

Now may He who supplies seed to the sower, and bread for food, supply and multiply the seed you have sown and increase the fruits of your righteousness.
(2 Corinthians 9:10)

God supplies seed to the sower and bread to the consumer. Most of us only know about the bread that God supplies, not the seed.

Four months into 2014, something broke open in our ministry. I remember that youth service when someone finally got saved. Then the next week, another person, and then another. It's was like a dam broke. We haven't had a week since then where someone doesn't get saved. At that time, healings started to flow, testimonies started to pour in, and deliverances started breaking out. The youth group exploded. And that year, we moved into our new home. I still don't know how it happened. We didn't have extra money. We were giving all of it every month. We continued to grow in generosity and continued to give $1,000 a month to different ministries. We started to give away cars and by God's grace, we've given over ten cars in ten years. I am not sharing this to brag, but to encourage you with how this divine truth has changed my life and ministry.

A year ago, when our congregation stepped into a new church-building phase, we had just sold our house, flipped some properties, and made some extra money that we were saving up to buy a dream home. But both of us felt inspired by the Holy Spirit that it was time to give all our savings to the building fund. Let me tell you, that was painful! It was our biggest sacrifice ever, but shortly after that, different people in our church started to give sacrificial offerings as well. A spirit of generosity broke out in our church. As of the time of this writing, I also decided to return my salary which the church board designated for me this past year, and by God's grace will continue to do as He provides.

It's About What We Have Left

The concept of sacrifice penetrates the entire Bible. Abel offered a sacrifice to God (Genesis 4:4). Noah offered a burnt offering to God after the flood (Genesis 8:20). Abraham was tested by God to sacrifice what he loved most—his son (Genesis 22). The Old Testament law prescribed five types of sacrifices, which can be broken into two categories: the "thank you offerings," which included grain offerings with other fellowship offerings, and the "I am sorry offerings," which were burnt offerings, sin offerings, and guilt offerings (Leviticus 1-6). The Hebrew word for sacrifice is *zabach*, and it means "to slaughter for sacrifice."[26] Sacrifice carried the idea of death on someone's behalf. These sacrifices were not to manipulate God for personal gain. They represented thankful responses to God's abundant blessings, effective forgiveness of sin, and restored fellowship between God and men.

In this church age, we don't have to offer animal sacrifices to earn God's forgiveness because Jesus effectively accomplished that on the Cross. By one sacrifice of His shed blood, He has perfected forever those who come to God through repentance and faith (Hebrews 10:10-14).

Three sacrifices continue to exist today. There is the "sacrifice of praise," according to Hebrews 13:15. Sometimes praising God really is a sacrifice, especially when you don't feel like doing it. But God is pleased when you praise and glorify Him in spite of your circumstances. There is the "living sacrifice of our bodies," according to Romans 12:1. God delights when you present your body as an instrument of righteousness, wholly and acceptable to Him. Being totally surrendered to Him is genuine worship. And finally, there is the "sacrifice of our finances." In Hebrews 13:16 the author said, "But do not forget to do good and to share, for with such sacrifices God is well pleased." God is well-pleased when we reflect His character of generosity. Augustine of Hippo, the great North African bishop, defined sacrifice as "the surrender of something of value for the sake of something else."

Sacrificial giving is giving to others beyond your financial means. Today's financial advisers and planners teach us to live within our means, and rightly so. Our generation lives way beyond their means, incurring immense credit card debt and heavy bank loans. But that is the very thing for which Paul praised the church in Macedonia.

For I bear witness that according to their ability, yes,
and beyond their ability, they were freely willing,

imploring us with much urgency that we would
receive the gift and the fellowship of the ministering
to the saints.

(2 Corinthians 8:3)

They were generous according to their ability and even gave beyond their ability, freely, willingly, even imploring with urgency that Paul would receive their gift. Now that's radical!

C.S. Lewis' observations on generosity pinch a bit. He wrote,

> "I do not believe one can settle how much we ought to give. I am afraid the only safe rule is to give more than we can spare. In other words, if our expenditure on comforts, luxuries, amusements, etc., is up to the standard common among those with the same income as ours, we are probably giving away too little. If our charities do not at all pinch or hamper us, I should say they [our expenditures] are too small. There ought to be things we should like to do and cannot do because our charities' expenditure excludes them."[27]

Sacrifice is not measured by what we give, but rather by what we have left over after we give. Jesus said the widow who gave two pennies into the temple coffers gave more than those who gave a lot, because she gave everything she had (Mark 12:41-44). This widow did not give from a surplus. There was nothing balanced or budgeted about her giving. It was not affordable. One could even say it was reckless to give her entire income. But it reflected an attitude of her total love for God and deep faith. There was nothing shallow or partial in the way she gave. Jesus noticed her radical giving and complimented her. Most of us would have advised her not to do that. Plus, let's not forget that she gave her offering to the temple, which was not entirely holy and righteous. Someone can make a case that she was giving to an unworthy place. But Jesus didn't view her giving like that at all. When Jesus compared her giving to others, He highlighted the way He measures our giving. True sacrifice is not what you give but what you have left. If someone gives five dollars and that's all they have to give, that's a painful sacrifice. Another person can give $5,000 and still have $50,000 left. Their $5,000 is only an offering, not a sacrifice. Remember, the chicken can give an egg without suffering; but to give bacon, the pig must give his all.

I define sacrificial giving as *giving until it hurts*. If your giving to the Lord does not "hurt" or infringe upon the comfort level of your lifestyle, then it's not sacrificial. If your giving does not stretch you and challenge your faith, then it most likely is not sacrificial. Not all giving has to be sacrificial, but we have to grow in the grace of God to practice sacrificial giving in our development as disciples of Jesus Christ.

Tithing is the Starting Point

I find it interesting that Jesus didn't focus too much on tithing in His teachings. He did correct the legalistic abuse of tithing, but tithing wasn't His main focus. I believe in and teach the practice of tithing, but I also believe that giving only ten percent of one's income misses the entire point. The Old Testament practice of tithing came way before God gave the Law to Moses. Abraham and Jacob practiced it some four hundred years earlier. This practice became law only after Israel came out of Egypt. The law of tithing was mainly a response to their deliverance from their slavery. Today, we live in response to Jesus' sacrificial death and our salvation. Our generosity is a response to God's gift of eternal salvation through faith.

The Old Testament law of tithing was focused primarily on maintaining the ministry of priests and Levites, and the maintenance work in the temple. The New Testament Church has the mission and vision to reach the world, not just to maintain our church buildings and pay for staff and utilities. Our generosity is to provide fuel for the mission of reaching the world for Jesus Christ. All our giving, tithing, or sacrifice is to fuel the great commission, whether through the local church that's winning souls, or supporting missionaries who are spreading the gospel.

Tithing alone misses the entire point of discipleship. Think about Jesus' approach: "He answered and said to them, "He who has two tunics, let him give to him who has none; and he who has food, let him do likewise" (Luke 3:11). The bar is pretty high. If you have two tunics and give one away, that is fifty percent of what you have, not just ten percent.

When Jesus entered Zacchaeus' house, the new convert declared, "Look, Lord, I give half of my goods to the poor; and if I have taken anything from anyone by false accusation, I restore fourfold" (Luke 19:8). Jesus' new disciple committed not to only giving ten percent to the poor, but he offered fifty percent of his wealth to them. And in repentance, he also made generous restitution of whatever he extorted from the taxpayers. That's radical and seems unreasonable at first, but Jesus didn't object to his generosity. Jesus didn't say, "Wait Zacchaeus, you don't need to do that." Instead, Jesus responded, "Today salvation has come to this house" (Luke 19:1-9).

It's hard to read books and articles about discipleship and reconcile how their teaching on the "tithing" model fits into what we see in the above verses. I am not opposed to tithing. I believe it's a good starting point, but real discipleship requires us to lay our whole life down and be one hundred percent available to the Lord. For a Christian, ten percent should be the floor, not the ceiling. It should be a place to begin, not a place to end. Even Paul urged followers of Jesus not only to be generous, but to excel in generosity.

> *But as you abound in everything—in faith, in speech, in knowledge, in all diligence, and in your love for us—see that you abound in this grace also.*
>
> (2 Corinthians 8:7)

Generosity is less about donations and more about discipleship.

> *So Jesus answered and said, "Assuredly, I say to you, there is no one who has left house or brothers or sisters or father or mother or wife or children or lands, for My sake and the gospel's."*
>
> (Mark 10:29)

Sacrifice for Jesus' sake and for the gospel's sake is what a true disciple signs up for. Our life ought not to be dearer to us than Jesus' life was to Him. The apostles and martyrs acted on this principle. We can either waste our life by holding on to it and wreck it by sin, or we can lay down our life for His cause. C.T. Studd, the British missionary, once said, "Only one life, 'twill soon be past, only what's done for Christ will last."

If you're afraid of losing your wealth and life's personal ambitions for Jesus' sake, I want to remind you that Jesus is worthy of everything you're afraid of losing. At the root of discipleship is sacrifice, death to self, a total surrender to His will.

Spiritually Rich

In building more spiritual fire on your altar, there is a lot more to "sacrifice" than you might realize. It's one of the essential sticks that you must put on the fire. Prayer fights pride. Fasting fights appetites. Giving fights greed. Money has a greater pull on your heart than food does because your heart follows your treasure. Giving redirects your heart. Jesus said, "...where your treasure is, there your heart will be also" (Matthew 6:21).

It doesn't say, "where your fasting is, there your heart will be." It also doesn't say, "where your prayer is, there is your heart." Nor does it say, "where your heart is, there will be your treasure." Treasure comes first. Heart *follows* treasure. You decide where to put your treasure, and your treasure will pull your heart in that direction. Augustine, one of the Latin fathers of the Church, said,

> "Where your pleasure is, there is your treasure;
> where your treasure is, there is your heart; where
> your heart is, there is your happiness."

The treasure that Jesus is talking about is more than just the financial source for your tithing or almsgiving. In Matthew 6, Jesus spoke about giving alms to the poor, praying in secret, and fasting before God. But then He turned His attention to the topic of your treasure (whatever you greatly value). He told us not to store them up here on earth, but to relinquish them into the spirit realm, which is called "heaven."

Giving up your material treasures to God can be painful. Sacrifice pinches the heart. If it does not pinch your heart, it will not move your heart. Sacrifice is giving what costs you, not what's convenient for you to give, and it's usually painful. It's not giving out of your surplus or what you have too much of.

It's not giving your leftovers to God. It's like Abraham giving up his beloved, promised son Isaac to God. He offered Isaac, not Ishmael. It's giving what we love, not what we don't need.

Jesus modeled a life of sacrifice and His disciples followed that example. They left home, family, and friends to follow Jesus. David was an example of an extravagant giver, having given over 100,000 talents of gold (about 3,365 tons) to the temple project. Converting that to today's gold value, it's worth about $200 billion. He also gave 1 million talents of silver (about 33,000 tons), equaling about $24 billion worth. That's a lot of money given to a temple-building project. And Mary is another example of generosity, giving up to a year's wages worth of perfume to pour over and anoint Jesus' feet.

When my wife and I started on the journey of radical generosity, I started to become more conscious of heaven. At first, I was concerned that maybe it was a sign that I was going to die soon. Perhaps the Lord was preparing me to leave this earth. I was in my late twenties and early thirties, a bit too early to die. I asked the Lord why I was being drawn to thinking about heaven so much. I know that the Scriptures tell us that heaven is our final home and our eternal hope, but I wasn't thinking about it so much until I started to give more.

The Holy Spirit gently responded to me during prayer and said: "For the first time, you have more treasure stored up here in heaven than there on earth, and therefore, your heart is gravitating toward where your treasure is." You know, if you put all your money into the stock market, you will be checking your stock market account daily. If you put your treasure in heaven, you will be thinking about heaven. Your heart follows your treasure.

A lot of us are so earthly-minded that we are not conscious of heaven or the heavenly realm, because our treasures are here on earth, not there. We let our roots grow too deeply into the visible, material, fading world. Jesus called the rich man a fool because he laid up treasure for himself on earth but was not rich toward God. Paul told Timothy to teach rich people "to be rich in good works" and store up for themselves a foundation for the time to come (1 Timothy 6:18-19).

Generosity contributes much, much more to your spiritual growth than you realize. The Bible has more verses on money than on faith and prayer combined. Nearly fifteen percent of everything Jesus taught was about money—more than on hell and heaven combined. One-third of His parables dealt with money. The only subject Jesus spoke about more than money was the Kingdom of God. Why is that? Money is a huge indicator of where our loyalties and devotion lie. Someone has said, "A checkbook is a theological document; it will tell you who and what you worship." Your bank statement tells what you believe.

As Christians, our net worth shouldn't determine our self-worth. We don't trust in riches, but we trust in our provider-God. We are not attached to our possessions. They don't own us–we own them. When the time comes to part with our possessions, we gladly do it. We are not owners, but only stewards or managers of what's been given to us. Giving comes easy when you consider that all you have is not yours.

Eternally Wealthy

Generosity causes us to transfer our resources from here to there. There is a humorous parable about a rich man going to heaven and meeting Peter at the pearly gates. He was expecting a mansion. Instead, Peter took him to a nice little shack that was not what the rich man was expecting. The rich man asked Peter, "I thought everyone gets a mansion in heaven." Peter responded to him, "We build the best type of house with the material you send." Even though it's not a true story, it does carry some truth in it.

> *But lay up for yourselves treasures in heaven, where neither moth nor rust destroys and where thieves do not break in and steal.*
>
> (Matthew 6:20)

We can store treasures in heaven, and those treasures will be ours for eternity. When we sow into God's kingdom, it all gets transferred to our heavenly account. In heaven, it gains huge interest.

> *And everyone who has left houses or brothers or sisters or father or mother or wife or children or lands, for My name's sake, shall receive a hundredfold, and inherit eternal life.*
>
> (Matthew 19:29)

Imagine having invested in Amazon, Apple, or Tesla when they first got started. Most likely, you missed that opportunity, but those companies come and go. God's kingdom is eternal; you will live forever. Be wise to invest into your eternal account. You shouldn't be concerned about storing more and more in your IRA (Individual Retirement Account), but more importantly, you need to plan and contribute to your IEA (Individual Eternity Account).

Remember, what leaves your hand does not leave your life. It gets transferred to your eternal account. In there, Jesus said no one can steal it. Inflation can't eat it. Satan can't touch it. Here on earth, our resources can be lost to bad investment, inflation, theft, and sometimes just demonic attacks on your finances. However, Satan can't steal what you gave to the Lord! He can't mess with your spiritual account.

John Maxwell, in his book *The 11 Essential Changes Every Leader Must Embrace*, tells a story about James and a few of his friends, who went out on a boat to fish for lobsters and succeeded in gathering a massive catch of 125 lobsters. When he got home, he had a freezer full of lobsters—more than enough to last him an entire year. The day after James got home, his friend Jeff dropped by his house, and James offered him a lobster. Jeff was delighted. This interaction with Jeff prompted him to ask himself, *Who else do I know that might enjoy getting a lobster?* James got so excited by the idea of giving lobsters to his friends, that by the end of the week, he had given away 122 lobsters, keeping only three for himself. He had such a great time giving that he didn't even mind that his supply had dwindled from a year's supply to only enough for one meal. Several days later, James went into his garage and was assaulted by a terrible stench. He followed his nose to the freezer and opened it to find that the electricity had gone out, and the remaining three lobsters he kept there had spoiled. As he cleaned up the mess, he felt sorry for himself. But then he remembered all the lobsters he had given away, and it gave him great joy. If he hadn't shared his bounty with others, all of it would have been wasted.

When it comes to living for eternity, John Wesley is such a great example of that. In the 1700s, he was a very important and active figure in the Evangelical Awakening in England. He worked very hard, teaching, preaching, writing, organizing events, and taking part in social causes. John Wesley made over £100,000 from the books he wrote, which would be equivalent to $10 million today. When he died, he had no money because he had given almost everything he had to help poor people, support Christian activities, and help other ministers. He dedicated his life, skills, and money to building up the Christian faith.

One of Wesley's most famous sermons is "The Use of Money." This sermon looked closely at Luke 16:9. Wesley said, "Gain all you can, save all you can, and give all you can." Here are the words of the conclusion of that sermon:

> "Gain all you can, without hurting either yourself or your neighbor, in soul or body, by applying hereto with unintermitted diligence, and with all the understanding which God has given you. Save all you can, by cutting off every expense which serves only to indulge foolish desire; to gratify either the desire of the flesh, the desire of the eye, or the pride of life; waste nothing, living or dying, on sin or folly, whether for yourself or your children. And then, give all you can, or, in other words, give all you have to God. Do not stint yourself...to this or that proportion. "*Render unto God*," not a tenth, not a third, not half, but all that is God's, be it more or less; by employing all on yourself, your household, the household of faith, and all mankind, in such a manner, that you may give a good account of your stewardship when ye can no longer be stewards."

Financially Blessed

Financial sacrifice not only brings spiritual wealth, and eternal riches, but also releases financial blessings. When it comes to financial prosperity, there are two extremes: the "prosperity" gospel, as some call it, and the "poverty" gospel. Neither of these are the gospel of Christ. Jesus had only one gospel–the gospel of the kingdom. In a nutshell, the prosperity gospel teaches that if you're righteous you will be rich, whereas the poverty gospel preachers claim that if you are poor, you are pious, because wealth is wicked. Every truth in God's Word can be abused. I don't believe in either the poverty or the prosperity gospel, but I do know that you can't outgive God, and the purpose of prosperity is that it be used as a means of serving God. Jesus said,

Give, and it will be given to you: good measure, pressed down, shaken together, and running over will be put into your bosom. For with the same measure that you use, it will be measured back to you.

(Luke 6:38)

Giving gives back. We don't give to get; we get to give. That's a principle that works.

In another place, Paul referred to giving as sowing.

But this I say: He who sows sparingly will also reap sparingly, and he who sows bountifully will also reap bountifully.

(2 Corinthians 9:6)

Everyone knows the basic principles of farming: You reap what you sow. You reap where you sow. You reap more than you sow. You reap only after you sow. Paul taught much on suffering and persecution, but he didn't shy away from teaching the principle that those who sow or give bountifully will also reap bountifully.

John Bunyan once said, "A man there was, and they called him mad; the more he gave, the more he had." I think every generous giver has experienced that. It can't be explained; it can only be experienced! Generosity teaches us that God is our source; our job is only a resource. If we don't practice it, we don't really believe that principle.

I have personally witnessed how sacrifice shifts seasons in your life. I have learned to give sacrificially, not to get money from God, but to be in step with His Holy Spirit. I have also witnessed how God has been faithful every time I've been obedient. Blessings come from obedience. Obedience sometimes is the greatest form of sacrifice. Once, my wife and I had a four-year plan to save up money to buy land and build a house, but instead, as mentioned at the beginning of this chapter, we gave it all to the Lord. I didn't expect anything back financially. In fact, I totally forgot about the house we wanted to build. And wouldn't you know, in less than twelve months, we moved into a new custom-built home next to the church. It was crazy. My wife and I were shocked at how it happened. It felt like Matthew 6:33 came alive in our life and all these things were indeed added to us.

Shortly before Covid hit, I launched a website to sell my books and audio sermons electronically. However, during a personal devotional time, the Lord clearly spoke to me to offer everything online for free. He said that in my ministry, He sent me people who needed my materials the most, but who couldn't afford to pay. He also promised that He would send people to finance the ministry. I obeyed right away. That week, I rented a

P.O. box for my ministry. The next day, I went to the box to try the key. On my way to the post office, I stopped to check how many times materials had been downloaded from my website in the previous twenty-four hours. Really, nobody knew who I was at that time, but I had 1,400 downloads. Wow! And to my greater surprise, when I opened my P.O. box, there was a check for exactly $1,400.00 waiting for me in an envelope. My P.O box address was not mentioned anywhere on the internet. I couldn't believe it! It's like God was saying, "Trust Me. I've got you." Since then, I have always offered my materials for free. God has been so faithful.

Recently, when we gave to the Lord our largest sacrifice, we gave our savings from the sale of the house and a few other things we had done on the side with real estate. We had plans to buy land where we could build our own house and live in it for the rest of our lives. The land we were looking for was either too expensive, or what we really wanted wasn't available. One month after that sacrifice, I also decided to relinquish the salary our church paid us. Shortly after that, someone called me and offered me some property to buy. It was ideal and exactly what my wife dreamed of having. God had spoken to this person to sell it and not keep it. Of course, we didn't have the necessary means to buy it. But, within a short period of time, all the funds came in. God provided!

I could go on and on about how many unexplainable things have happened in the area of finances since I started to obey God in sacrifice. Again, I want to declare that I don't believe this is a "give-one-thousand-to-get-ten-thousand" gimmick. I emphasize once again: we don't give to get; we get to give. The Bible prioritizes hard work, planning, and good stewardship, and giving is not the only financial principle the Scripture highlights. Truly our God is still the God who pours out manna in the wilderness, feeds a prophet from the beaks of ravens, and causes the oil bottle and flour bin to not go empty (Exodus 16; 1 Kings 17:4-6; 2 Kings 4:1-7; 1 Kings 17:9-16). He is the God of more than enough! He can multiply bread and fish for you and guide you to find money for taxes in a fish's mouth (Matthew 17:27).

I once read a testimony of Robert G. LeTourneau. He was born into a Christian family on November 30, 1888. At first, he rejected the gospel, but then at sixteen, he came to Jesus. At thirty, he dedicated himself to being God's businessman. Robert designed and built machines and implements beyond the imagination of ordinary men. He introduced the rubber tire into the earthmoving and material handling industry, which is almost universally accepted today. He invented and developed the electric wheel. He pioneered the welding of various metals. His gigantic, mobile offshore drilling platforms support machinery that drill for undersea petroleum reserves around the world. In addition to all this, he showed his concern for the gospel witness by establishing regular chapel services for his employees and by employing three full-time chaplains in his manufacturing plants.

The LeTourneau University, which he and his wife founded, may well prove to be one of his greatest accomplishments as his influence has multiplied and spread throughout the world by dedicated Christian young people who have studied at the university. He started a monthly publication, *NOW*, which reached 600,000 people during his lifetime and circled the world with its message.

Robert traveled the world as a witnessing Christian businessman. He was the maker of nearly three hundred inventions and had hundreds of patents in his lifetime. And as he succeeded financially, he increased his giving to the point where he was giving ninety percent of his income to the Lord's work! He reversed tithing by giving ninety percent back into God's kingdom and living on just ten percent. He once said, "I shovel [money] out, and God shovels it back... but God has a bigger shovel!" I love this! God definitely has a bigger shovel.

In conclusion, I would like to add that God is not against us having wealth, but He is against wealth having us. Abraham was the father of faith and a friend of God, yet he was very rich. David was a man after God's heart, yet he was rich. Heaven is made of gold and very expensive material, yet it is the holy dwelling of God. The Bible condemns wealth in three areas: love for it (1 Timothy 6:10), trusting in it (Mark 10:23-24), and obtaining it the wrong way (Ephesians 4:28).

As prayer defeats pride, and fasting defeats lust, giving releases us from the grip of greed. We are only temporarily separated from whatever we give for Jesus' sake. It will go into our heavenly account. Remember, whatever you hold onto tightly is yours only temporarily; you will lose it permanently in eternity. Money is a good means, but a bad master. Don't let money possess you. The goal is to serve Jesus with your money.

Don't worship money; worship God with your money. Don't fear losing what you can't keep, because Jesus is worthy of everything you are afraid of losing. Fear God more than you fear losing money because, no matter what, you're going to leave it all behind. It has been said that no one has ever seen a U-Haul trailer attached to a hearse. You can't take anything with you, but you can send it on ahead. Sacrificial giving is something that the Lord will prompt you to do when your life is on fire for the Lord.

CHAPTER 12

Viper Attacks

When I was a teen in Ukraine, we used to play soccer on my street almost every day. We didn't have video games, TV, or even board games. We had a soccer ball and a neighbor's back yard. Soccer would bring the best and the worst out of all of us. Sometimes it felt like we needed to get saved again after the game! At times, our emotions ran high. A few times, we even got into physical fights over the stupid game.

The basic idea of soccer is that there are two opposing teams who want to win. Once you get the ball, your team does all they can to help you succeed. Likewise, the opposing team does all they can to make you lose the ball. You may be reading this and thinking I am explaining sports to toddlers. But here is my point: The other team doesn't attack you until you get the ball. The only time the opposing team stops attacking you is when you lose the ball or you score the goal.

That is how it works with our Christian life. I want you to know that we are on the winning team—Jesus' team. God has tons of people, angels, and the Holy Spirit helping you to win. The path to victory isn't easy because there is an opposing team; it's called the kingdom of darkness. The kingdom of our enemy doesn't mind you as long as you don't have the ball (a fire and an assignment from God). If you're cold, complacent, comfortable, compromising, or a carnal Christian, you are not a threat to the enemy. He doesn't waste his time attacking your fire because you are already in his trap. It's when you get the ball—get on fire—that you are a headache for the devil. You have the potential to turn the world upside down. You are going to win souls, which means he will lose them. This is why Christians get attacked after they get on fire. The enemy is threatened by us, so he does everything he can to try to stop us.

Surviving the Storm Only to be Bitten by a Snake

Let's get back to Paul on the island of Malta. When we left off, they had started a fire and Paul was busy bringing sticks to keep it burning. Just when things got good and warm, a viper appeared. Some believe it was the *vipera aspis* snake, which is partial to wood. Today, it is extinct on the island of Malta, probably because the wood has been removed from the island. Coming out of the bundles of sticks Paul had gathered, it went for his hand. It didn't just attack him and fall back into the fire; it fastened to his hand. Luke, the writer of the book of Acts, didn't mention if it was a poisonous snake. But it's interesting that the islanders thought it was a deadly snake; they expected Paul to drop dead. However, Paul didn't drop dead; he dropped the snake into the flames.

As Paul was under attack from the snake, those around him began to gossip. It's funny how that happened. We experience this today—the moment we are under attack, people start talking. The islanders knew Paul survived a shipwreck, but then he was attacked by a snake. They concluded that the gods were paying him back for some evil he had done. Whispers were going around, and Paul was getting what he deserved. When Paul dropped the snake into the fire and nothing happened to him, everyone changed their mind. At that point, Paul was no longer a murderer deserving of death—he was a god. How quickly their opinions changed! But obviously, both of their conclusions about Paul were wrong.

Fire Exposes

Let's talk a little more about snakes. In Paul's case, a snake was there among the wood and the heat made it uncomfortable enough that it had to leave. Did you catch that? It was the heat that made the snake uncomfortable.

> *A viper came out because of the heat...*
>
> (Acts 28:3)

Snakes love to stay hidden, but fire always exposes them. Fire pushes them out into the open. Sometimes people ask me how to bring deliverance to the church. How do you make demons stop hiding? My response is to increase the heat. Demons hate fire. They can't stand the anointing. When I say "fire," I don't mean more passion, enthusiasm, or hype. Demons aren't threatened by passion but by power. It's not eloquent speaking skills that cause them to come out; it's the name of Jesus Christ.

When you start building fire in your spiritual life, don't be surprised if snakes start coming out. Fire doesn't bring the snakes; it simply exposes them. Vipers were always there hiding; you just didn't know it. Fire made them uncomfortable for the first time. Those who start getting deeper in the Lord sometimes get discouraged when they encounter these types of attacks. Some believers choose to put out the fire to stop the vipers. This is the wrong solution! It's like playing straight into the enemy's hands. The fire is not the problem; the snakes are the problem. Kill the snakes, but continue to fuel the fire. Push through the attacks until the enemy is the one that's defeated, not you.

If you started to get attacked after you came to Jesus, Jesus isn't your problem—demons are. Those demons have most likely been there for generations because no one annoyed them. Until you started to build a fire, they were operating undetected behind the scenes. Now is not the time to put out the fire; it's time to let the fire burn, force the snake out of hiding, and crush his head!

Attacks From the Outside

Please understand that in this chapter we are dealing with demonic attacks, not natural or bad circumstances, or even persecution for our faith. Also, it's important to differentiate between being demonized and being attacked by demons. To be "demonized" means you have demons living in you. Yes, that can happen to Christians as well. For more explanation on this subject, please go to my YouTube channel. When demons are on the inside, they torment, harass, entice, enslave, cause addictions, and attack the physical body. Those demons must be expelled—cast out! We call that "deliverance"—removing demons from the inside. It's kind of like eviction. Deliverance is getting demons out of the person, not getting demons off the person. I know it is very popular in charismatic circles to get demons off of a person, but it's not in the Bible. Demons come *out* of a person, not *off* of a person.

After a person gets delivered (or if a person didn't have demons on the inside), he or she can still experience attacks from demons. Those attacks from the outside are different than attacks from the inside. The first big difference is that demons are not inside. It's like having mosquitoes inside the house versus having them outside of the house. Or like having rain inside the house because you have a hole in the roof, versus having rain outside of the house. When they are on the outside, they can't control you; but they can still attack you. Sometimes demons attack to make an open door; other times, they attack simply because they are demons—they are here to deceive, steal, kill, and destroy.

The second big difference with having demons on the outside is that they claim to be on the inside. I want you to know their tactic: When they are on the inside, they rarely seek to make themselves known. They love to stay hidden. The moment you get delivered, and they are on the outside, they will whisper lies to you and say they are still on the inside. This can create confusion in the mind of a person who was delivered. Let me emphasize that they can't control you anymore. They are like the Egyptians who pursued Israel after their deliverance. They were the same Egyptians and the same Israelites, but the dynamic was not the same anymore. The Israelites were free, and the Egyptians were no longer in control of them. They tried to intimidate and recapture Israel, but failed miserably. They used the same tactic that demons use. Demons on the outside are doomed to fail if you are determined to go forward with God and exercise your authority.

The third difference between inside attacks and outside attacks is the correct response. For example, if you have demons on the inside of you, you need deliverance. If you have demons on the outside, you need to exercise dominion. Let me state it again: Demons on the inside need to be removed, but demons on the outside need to be resisted. Think of Egypt and Canaan (the Promised Land). Israel needed to be delivered from Egypt, but the Promised Land needed to be conquered. God sent Moses to lead the Israelites out of Egypt, but He empowered them to get enemies out of the Promised Land. In Egypt, they were slaves; in the Promised Land, they were soldiers. That's a big difference! For demonic attacks on the outside, you don't need deliverance; you need to practice dominion. You don't need someone to cast them out for you; you need to shake them off.

> *Therefore submit to God. Resist the devil and he will flee from you.*
>
> (James 4:7)

Every person who gets delivered needs to learn how to walk in their authority, resisting the enemy by using the Word of God, and putting on the whole armor of God. I previously wrote a book on this topic called *Fight Back*. You can learn more about how to use your authority and walk in dominion through that book.

Shake it Off

The problem with the viper, as with any snake, was that it fastened itself to Paul's hand. It attached itself and took hold of Paul's hand. The snake was persistent and determined. There are demonic spirits that operate just like that. They grasp, seize, and attach themselves to us for our destruction. This can also come in the form of a spiritual attack, nightmares, and attacks on our mind. Everyone who is going through a viper attack will know in their spirit that what they are experiencing is not normal. It's a spiritual attack.

Please understand, snakes must be handled differently than storms. We survive storms, but we must shake off snakes. Storms we endure; snakes we conquer. Vipers must be confronted. Think back to when Israel attacked enemies when occupying the Promised Land. God didn't drive them out for them; Israel drove them out with God's help. In fact, Israel only got as much land as they were willing to fight for, which was not as much as God had promised them. Even Jesus, when He was in the wilderness being tempted by the devil, confronted him. He didn't pray to God to silence the devil; He shook off that snake by quoting the Scripture, which is something very practical that you can do, too. Speak to the enemy! It sounds weird, but it's biblical. Jesus did that.

When the snake attacks you, it usually happens in your mind. Don't fight demonic thoughts with godly thoughts; fight demonic thoughts with spoken words from the Bible—out loud—that's how Jesus did it. It's good to memorize Bible verses to use during spiritual combat. God's Word is the sword of the Spirit (Ephesians 6:17). The sword referenced in Ephesians speaks of a small dagger for close combat. It means that when the enemy attacks from the outside, close to you, just stab him with the dagger. I apologize for the violent, graphic picture, but you get the point.

Sometimes you have to speak to the devil directly and tell him to get behind you, just as Jesus did. Other times, you quote the Word to combat his lies. Simply praying for God to silence the enemy is not how snakes get defeated. Paul shook off the snake; he didn't wait for God to intervene, nor did he pray for

God to kill the snake. God gave that authority to Paul. He gave that authority to you, too.

By the way, don't plan to die if you get bitten. Battle the snake that bit you. Even if the snake is fastened onto you and doesn't want to leave, don't quit. The devil will flee if you resist him (James 4:7). Have persistence, and he will give up. Even if you have fallen back into the sin that you got delivered from, repent, and get right back up.

> For a righteous man may fall seven times and rise
> again, but the wicked shall fall by calamity.
> (Proverbs 24:16)

Righteous people stumble and delivered people fall, but they get back up. It's been said that people don't drown by falling into water, they drown by staying there. If you fell into the same sin, repent, renounce it, remove yourself from that place, and resist the enemy.

One more thing I want to highlight in Paul's story is that when he was attacked by the viper, those around him assumed it was punishment for his sins. They concluded that he was a murderer. By the way, they weren't totally wrong—Paul did have a bad past—he had spent years persecuting Christians. Even though we don't see any mention of him killing believers himself, he did wreak havoc in their lives. But the Scripture does not say the viper attacked him because God was punishing him for his sins. Instead, Paul threw that viper into the fire and the natives on the island were astonished.

Fire Kills

When God created mankind, He placed them in the Garden of Eden. He blessed them and told them to be fruitful, multiply, and have dominion (Genesis 1:28). People were created to live in God's presence and to walk in dominion. God never created us for deliverance, but for dominion. Once we lost God's presence, we lost dominion. I want to be clear: dominion doesn't work without devotion. One of the reasons trying to walk in dominion doesn't work is because we don't live in devotion to God. Walking in authority won't work if we are not under the authority of the lordship of Jesus Christ.

I tell people all the time, "You can't shake your snake into my fire." You must build your own flame where you can drop the snake. That is how you walk in dominion. Deliverance is different. A man or woman of God who carries the fire of God can bring deliverance for you, but if you want to walk in dominion, you must cultivate your own fire. You must throw the snake into your fire. Obviously, you can come to the pastor or revivalist to pray for you, but if you want to be effective at killing vipers, you must have your own flame. You can only shake the snake into your own fire.

As I mentioned earlier in the book, when we get a fever, it is the body's natural defense system against infection. The higher temperature helps your body fight off the infection more effectively. In the same way, when you're under spiritual attack, you must increase the spiritual temperature to fight it. The enemy can't stand the heat. Demons are tormented by fire. That's why you need your life to be on fire—so that when snakes attack, you'll have a place to throw them. Those who don't have a prayer life, don't read the Scriptures, and don't fast, give, or go to church, find it difficult to walk in authority.

Condemn Condemnation

I believe one of the strongest weapons the enemy has is his voice that comes into our thoughts—the voice of doubt, fear, and condemnation. In fact, the devil didn't physically attack Eve, he simply spoke to her. His voice was his weapon. The enemy couldn't create any vice until his voice was acted upon. Hearing the voice of the Enemy doesn't make you sinful, but heeding it brings you under his influence. Both Eve and Jesus heard the voice of the Enemy. Eve acted on it; Jesus attacked it. Don't heed every voice you hear or imagine. Demonic voices must be condemned.

One of the strongest voices of the enemy we will hear is the voice of condemnation. The devil brings up our past to add volumes of condemnation. I noticed that when the devil brings up your past, it's because he ran out of new material with which to attack you. Someone once said that if the devil brings up your past, you should bring up his future. I like that. God forgives our sins, but the guilt associated with our sin doesn't leave us right away. If there was a fire in your house, it created smoke. Let's say you put the fire out. There's no more fire, but the smoke lingers for some time. It's not until you open the windows and doors that it will leave—slowly. For some of us, that describes our battle with guilt, shame, and condemnation. We know that God has forgiven us, but we hear demonic voices reminding us of our mistakes, faults, and shortcomings. What can we do?

We can condemn condemnation. Yes, we must confront it because, in Christ, there is no condemnation (Romans 8:1). That means the smoke has to go. The prophet Isaiah spoke a powerful promise that you probably have heard or even quoted:

No weapon formed against you shall prosper, and every tongue which rises against you in judgment you shall condemn.

(Isaiah 54:17)

No weapon shall prosper. We usually stop at that. But then it says that every tongue that rises against you in judgment you shall condemn. When voices of condemnation rise against you—judging you—you can condemn them. You can confront them. Silence those voices. I believe the devil's weapons are only as powerful as his voice. If he can't get his voice into your head, he will have a hard time getting his vices to operate in your life.

How can we condemn condemnation? Well, later in that same verse, the prophet Isaiah told us:

This is the heritage of the servants of the LORD, and their righteousness is from Me.

(Isaiah 54:17)

First of all, we are God's children. Second, our righteousness is from God. Let me emphasize that our righteousness doesn't come from our works, but from God. So, if the devil comes to you saying you're not good enough, you failed, your past is terrible, you're washed up, you're never going to make it, etc., just tell him, "I am God's child; my righteousness doesn't come from my past but by Jesus' blood." Jesus said to the woman caught in the act of adultery,

Neither do I condemn you; go and sin no more.

(John 8:11)

He says the same thing to everyone who comes to Him in faith and repentance. You can't *go and sin no more* if you don't believe the promise that, in Jesus, there is no condemnation. If you're struggling with repeated sin, hear me, please—the devil's goal is to keep you in condemnation. Sin is not his goal, condemnation is. Your sinful act doesn't last long, but guilt can last a very long time. As long as you wallow in condemnation and guilt, he is beating you. Jesus promises forgiveness and freedom from guilt. Life without condemnation doesn't mean we are sinless; it means we *sin less*. Condemnation empowers sin, but freedom from condemnation enables holiness. After I wash my car, I avoid puddles on the road so I can keep my car clean. If my car is not clean, I will be honest, I don't avoid any puddles—I love the splash it makes! The same principle applies to holiness. If we are condemned, we will compromise; if we are free from condemnation, we are free to walk according to our convictions.

CHAPTER 13

Calling in Chains

The five American men who were killed by the Waodani tribe in Ecuador in 1956 came to be known as "The Five Martyrs of the Upper Amazon." Jim Elliot, Nate Saint, Ed McCully, Peter Fleming, and Roger Youderian were all Christian missionaries who belonged to an organization called Summer Institute of Linguistics (SIL) and were attempting to make contact with the Waodani people, who were considered to be one of the most violent and isolated tribes in the Amazon.

Missionaries had been trying to make peaceful contact with the tribe for some time, using a plane to drop gifts and messages to them. Their efforts were not successful, and the tribe's hostility toward outsiders was well known in the area. On January 8, 1956, the five men set out in a plane to make contact on the ground with the Waodani. They landed on the beach with more gifts but were suddenly and brutally speared to death.

The tragedy caused a sensation in the United States, and the story of the martyrs was widely reported in the media. The deaths of the five men were a turning point in the history of missions to the tribe, and their story inspired many others to continue the work they began.

The wives of these five men were left behind and decided to continue their husbands' work. Eventually, they were able to establish peaceful relations with the Waodani tribe and share the gospel with them. The story of these five martyrs was later chronicled in the book, *Through Gates of Splendor,* by Elisabeth Elliot. It went on to become a best seller and was made into a movie as well.[28]

One of the quotes from Jim Elliot, who was speared to death, that has inspired my faith is, "He is no fool who gives what he cannot keep to gain what he cannot lose."

I want to open a veil to a side of ministry that we seldom see. Serving God has its perks, but it also comes with a price. Anyone who has a great calling from God must make a shift from the benefits of the ministry to the cost. For Jim Elliot, ministry wasn't about perks, but the price that he paid with his life.

While some ministers will be entrusted by God with popularity, prosperity, and a large platform, we must understand that all those things are tests and responsibilities more than rewards. The danger is when we see a few of those examples and conclude that's what ministry is supposed to look like. Christian leadership is about servanthood, not being a celebrity. Jesus came to serve, not to be served (Mark 10:45). Jesus is the ultimate example of ministry, not a pastor who is a best-selling author and has a million followers on Instagram. Jesus washed His disciples' feet and then asked them to do the same (John 13:3-17). Ministry is more about the towel than the title. By the way, servanthood is not about slavery. Servanthood is voluntary; it's motivated from within by God's love. It's not mandated by insistence, manipulation, pressure, guilt, or demand. We must remove every wrong concept of what it means to serve God.

Let's clarify a few things. Careers and callings are different. Careers are decided; callings are discovered. Careers are natural; callings are supernatural. Careers can change; callings don't change. Every Christian has a specific calling. We have our general calling, which we should focus on, and as we fulfill our general calling, our specific calling will become more evident. We are all called to follow Jesus, forsake the world, and fish for souls. As we do that, our specific calling will become evident with time.

But one thing is certain: For everyone who is walking worthy of their calling, it will cause them pain. Now, I don't want to scare anyone away from doing ministry, but I do want you to count the cost. Two main sources of the pain that comes with ministry are responsibility and relationships. Responsibility deals with pressure that comes from the position a person holds. Relational pain comes from people. Pressure and people. There is a great book on this subject called *Leadership Pain* by Dr. Sam Chand. Here is one of his quotes that summarizes this well:

> "The best leaders had to endure more pain. Many people could never have more influence because they don't have a big enough leadership pain threshold. If you are not hurting, you are not leading. Reluctance to face pain is your greatest limitation. There is no growth without change, no change without loss, and no loss without pain."[29]

The Viper Attacked What God Planned to Use

Paul was on the island, having survived the storm and the shipwreck. He shook the snake off and into the fire. He spent three months on that island. While he was there, God used him to bring revival. A leading citizen of Malta, Publius, was the main person in charge of the island (like a mayor). Publius' father was sick with a fever, and despite Paul's own troubles, he went and stretched out his hands to heal this man.

> *Paul went in to him and prayed, and he laid his hands*
> *on him and healed him.*
>
> (Acts 28:8)

After Publius's dad was healed, well, everyone wanted in on the action.

> *So when this was done, the rest of those on the island*
> *who had diseases also came and were healed.*
>
> (Acts 28:9)

I want you to notice that when Paul laid hands on Publius' dad, God healed him. How is that significant? It was the very same hand that the viper attacked. The snake attacked what God intended to use. God wanted Paul's hands to heal the sick; the viper wanted that hand to get infected and become useless. I wonder how many times that's the case in our own life. The devil attacks areas God wants to use. When I was in my teen years, struggling with porn, I felt so terrible and guilty that I even doubted my own salvation. I questioned if God would ever use a messed-up kid like me. Looking back at that time, after I was delivered, I see that the enemy kept attacking me with porn, not because I was the worst person who lived, but maybe the devil knew that God had a plan for my life and wanted to stop it. Sometimes I think the devil is a better judge of what God wants to do with us than we are. While we are in our infancy—young, immature, and unstable—he throws his best shots to take us out.

If you are under attack right now, take courage. Don't give in. Take a stand. Shake off those demonic lies and thoughts. Break those strongholds. Put on the shield of faith to defend yourself from the fiery darts of the devil (Ephesians 6:16). The story that really encouraged me in my time of attack was David dealing with the lion when it attacked his sheep. David privately battled a lion and a bear who tried to steal his sheep (1 Samuel 17:34-36). Instead of settling for defeat, he went after them. He killed those predators and rescued the sheep.

The Lord used that example to build my faith, teaching me that lions attack privately (for me, those lions came in the form of porn). The Lord taught me to fight them privately, and by doing so, He prepared me to fight "Goliaths" publicly through deliverance ministry. Every giant-killer is prepared in the wilderness by facing lions. Take courage—the enemy's attacks might be a sign that God has plans for you. The hand the snake bit was the hand God used. But, I also want to mention, if you're not heavily attacked, it doesn't mean God isn't going to use you!

Chains Don't Cancel Calling

Let's keep in mind that while on the island of Malta, Paul was still a prisoner. His case didn't get dismissed. His record wasn't cleared. He was still in the custody of the Roman centurion, on the way to Rome to await trial. But none of that stopped Paul from ministering to others. He could have made an excuse: *How can I serve others if I am in chains?* But he didn't waste time; he started a revival while he was still a prisoner.

You may have heard the statement, "You can't give away what you don't have." It usually means that if you are not personally doing very well, you should stay away from ministering to others. While there is some truth in that, I want to present another side of ministry that involves ministering out of God's Spirit more than your own well-being or understanding. Paul didn't let his chains intimidate him. And they surely didn't limit the Holy Spirit.

Let me also remind you that the first mention of healing in the Bible was when Abraham prayed for barren women (Genesis 20:17). Keep in mind, at the same time, Abraham's wife remained barren. Abraham didn't minister healing out of what he had experienced. It was sheer obedience to God's command. Surprisingly, God healed the women that Abraham prayed for, but his own wife was still barren (but not for long). Sometimes it's easier to minister healing than receive healing. Abraham didn't let the barrenness of his wife stop him from praying for healing for barren women.

Let me also remind you of Job, who prayed for his friends while he was still sick (Job 42:10). It was after that prayer that the Lord started to restore Job. Again, he ministered while in misery. He served others while suffering. He didn't let his pain stop him from God's purpose.

And, once there was a slave girl who was captured by the Syrian army and served the commander's wife. She shared about the healing power of God to her mistress, whose husband (Naaman) was a leper. Most people would have been hesitant to tell someone about God's power when God hadn't protected them from invaders. The young girl didn't care. As a result, Naaman was healed and worshipped God (2 Kings 5:1-19).

Here is another example: Joseph interpreted dreams for prisoners while in jail (Genesis 40-41). On top of all that, Joseph's own dreams from God had yet to be fulfilled. Instead of saying to others, "I don't believe in dreams anymore since God seems to have to let me down," he positioned himself to receive divine interpretation from God on behalf of others. In fact, this is the first time we see the gift of interpretation of dreams operating in Joseph's life. While he was helping others in jail, his own dreams seemed dead. It's funny how God works—we ourselves want gifts to flow when everything is awesome, but God chooses to develop His calling in the most unlikely places, times, and circumstances. If God is not threatened by our situations, we shouldn't be either.

Jesus is my final example. In the garden of Gethsemane, He healed the High Priest's servant's ear that Peter had cut off (Luke 22:51). Imagine that miracle, while He was being arrested! He could have simply put a sign on the door that said, "Healing ministry is not available anymore." Plus, the guy whose ear got cut off probably deserved it. He was coming to arrest Jesus! We don't even see him asking for healing. No, Jesus didn't stop healing others when He Himself was hurting. While hanging on the Cross, taking on the sin of the whole world, the man next to Him decides to get saved (Luke 23:33-43). Imagine that. This sinner waited until the end to get right with God. Jesus didn't respond to him, "Hey you, this is not a good time; I am kind of busy dying for the sins of the world—sorry man." No, Jesus saved him right then and there, while He was on the Cross.

Our Lord Jesus didn't stop ministering to others—even while He was suffering. And it doesn't stop there. As He hung on the Cross, He took care of His mom by asking His disciple John to take her in and provide for her (John 19:26-27). We should stop using our pain as an excuse. Yes, we need time to hear God and to heal, but stopping all service to others so we can focus on our personal pain might not be the best way to recover. It's been said, "Life is like tennis; those who serve well seldom lose." You too, can serve your way out of your struggle.

You Don't Need a Platform, You Need a Problem

On the island of Malta, Paul didn't have a video camera to stream, a microphone to preach, or a podium for the Torah. There was no church building, no title given to Paul or position for him to fill, and there was no platform for him. But the power of God wasn't restricted by the lack of a platform. It flowed beautifully through a yielded vessel. Paul did have his voice and his hands, and there were sick people. If you are called and anointed, you don't need a title—you need a towel. You don't need a microphone to minister to people; pick up your towel and go serve somebody. And you don't need a spotlight because *you* are the light. Find a dark place to shine.

We need to seek a problem to solve, not a platform to shine on. God's power works to heal the sick, cleanse the lepers, raise the dead, and drive out demons. That means we will see sickness, leprosy, dead people, and demons. We need problems to solve—unless, of course, we are not called or anointed. We may simply be ambitious due to an orphan spirit that seeks to use ministry to fix personal insecurities or daddy issues. If we look to ministry for validation, that will be the end of us. The call of God is to serve others, not serve ourselves. We're not in it for us, but for God and others. I hear many people complain that their pastors didn't give a place for them to preach, sing, or practice their gifts. That is the wrong approach.

No one is stopping you from going to the jail, the homeless shelter, under the bridge, to the park, or to the mall to serve. Also, in the world of the internet, no one is stopping you from going live on Instagram and praying for people. The church is not here to build you a platform. You owe it to God and the world to use every bit of the anointing you have to serve hurting people and snatch them off the highway to hell.

This reminds me of Stephen in the early church. He was appointed to be a deacon, helping to distribute food to the widows. Stephen had a great resumé: He was full of faith and the Holy Spirit, full of power, and he did great signs and wonders among the people (Acts 6:5, 8). This brother could preach! The longest sermon in the book of Acts is Stephen's. Interestingly, in the church, he was appointed as a deacon (food giveaway coordinator), not a preaching pastor. It seemed like his potential was greater than his position. His anointing was greater than his responsibility at church. Yet, that didn't stop Stephen from moving in signs and wonders on the streets—preaching his heart out—outside of the four walls of the church. Purpose doesn't need a platform; it needs people who have problems. God's anointing doesn't need a title or position. The power of God is like water; it doesn't need an open door. Water can flow into a room through a crack.

Serving is Not a Stepping Stone

Paul had a revival on the island of Malta, yet that didn't improve his condition. They received honor and provision from the natives, but Paul was still a prisoner: "They also honored us in many ways; and when we departed, they provided such things as were necessary" (Acts 28:10).

I want to address the notion that, *If I will be faithful, I will be promoted out of the place where I am serving to a higher place*. It's true that some people experience that. Some youth pastors become lead pastors. Some leaders become pastors. The Bible even says that God will reward us for our faithfulness, but that promise is referring to rewards in heaven. If we are serving with our eyes on a promotion, that means we are treating our calling as a career. Christian ministry is not a corporate ladder we climb.

Serving in the church as a stepping stone to a greater position reveals our motive: We are not actually serving people; we are using them as an opportunity to climb higher. We can use people to build ourselves a platform. The Bible compares Christians to the members of the human body (1 Corinthians 12:12-27). We don't promote the heart to be on the top of the head because of its faithfulness in pumping blood. The effectiveness of one organ doesn't automatically guarantee that it will be climbing a ladder to greater visibility. Those organs fulfill their duty without being visible or even recognized, which can be a scary thought.

The parts of my body that are not visible are still valuable. Value is not determined by visibility. A believer working in children's church is just as valuable as the pastor preaching on the pulpit. Using your current place of ministry as an opportunity to build a resumé so you can finally move up may be a great career move, but that concept is not found in the Bible. Again, ministry is not a career; it's a calling. Not every principle from the business world will apply in the kingdom. The Bible describes us as a body, not a business.

I am not saying that God doesn't develop us behind the scenes and then take us to the place where we are most suited for His purpose. David was a shepherd but then became a military leader and ruler over the nation. He was a musician in the palace and then became the king in the palace. There was a process.

God does have a process for developing His ministers into who He's called them to be. The problem happens when our motive and focus is no longer on God and His people, but on our own desired destination. We get so sick with "destination disease" that we miss the real reason we are in the ministry—to serve.

In this book, we have explored Paul's journey in terms of the storm, the shipwreck, and the snake bite, but we've also learned practical tools to overcome persecution, hardships, and demonic attacks. I want you to know that you are not alone in what you're going through. You're going to rise up. By faith, you're going to make it. By faith, all the witnesses in heaven made it. Heaven is cheering you on. I am praying for you now, but most importantly, Jesus lives to always make intercession for you.

> *Seeing then that we have a great High Priest who has passed through the heavens, Jesus the Son of God, let us hold fast our confession. For we do not have a High Priest who cannot sympathize with our weaknesses, but was in all points tempted as we are, yet without sin. Let us therefore come boldly to the throne of grace, that we may obtain mercy and find grace to help in time of need.*
>
> (Hebrews 4:14-16)

May you be victorious in every battle. May you prosper. May sickness be far from you. May your fire always burn. May the fruit of the Holy Spirit in your life be visible and feed the people around you. May you be strengthened in faith, enlightened with a deeper revelation of God, and glorify His name on the earth. In Jesus' name. Amen!

Heaven: Future Home, Present Hope

I once read a story about a missionary couple, Mr. & Mrs. Henry Morrison, who served for decades in Africa. After their missionary work, they returned to New York to retire. Like many missionaries, they had no retirement fund waiting for them, and their health was failing. They were tired, sick, and discouraged.

It happened that they were on the same ship as President Theodore Roosevelt, who was returning home from his hunting trip in Africa. Of course, everyone was watching the president; no one paid attention or cared about this old missionary couple. The missionary's wife grumbled that it was not fair that they gave their whole life in service to God, yet no one cared about them, while the president went on a fun trip, and there was much fanfare made about him.

When the ship docked in New York City, the news media, the mayor, dignitaries, and a band welcomed the president home;

but there was no one there for the missionary couple. They found a simple place to rest, and the wife went on to lament to the Lord the next day about how no one was there to welcome them. She told the Lord how bitter she felt seeing the president receive that kind of warm homecoming, while she and her husband arrived alone. When she finished complaining, it seemed as though the Lord put His hand on her shoulder and simply said, "BUT YOU ARE NOT HOME YET."

Rejoice for Heaven's Sake

Jesus told us to not only endure persecution, but to rejoice in the midst of it.

> *Rejoice and be exceedingly glad, for great is your reward in heaven, for so they persecuted the prophets who were before you.*
>
> (Matthew 5:12)

The motive for that joy is a reward in heaven. We don't rejoice because we love pain and suffering. Nor do we enjoy persecution for the sake of persecution; we endure persecution for the sake of heaven. When we think about where we are going, our hearts are filled with hope and joy. I remember when I was living in Ukraine as a child, and we were getting ready to emigrate to the U.S.A. My joy increased, not because life in Ukraine got easier, but because of the hope of where I was headed. There's something about where you're going that increases your joy:

> *Looking for the blessed hope and glorious appearing of our great God and Savior Jesus Christ.*
>
> (Titus 2:13)

Heaven is called our blessed hope.

Focusing too much on what we are going through can produce a victim mentality. We will begin to lick our wounds in self-pity, feel sorry for ourselves, and complain about how life is not fair and God is not helping us. Let me tell you that the way to heaven is full of roses that have thorns. The path to the promised land flowing with milk and honey is paved with persecution, a terrifying Red Sea, and fiery serpents. But you must not lose sight of the promised land. Don't let what you are suffering steal your focus, because it could hijack your joy. "Rejoice for great is your reward in heaven" requires one to lift his eyes from his present misery and fix them on heaven (Matt. 5:12). Jesus tells us not to be troubled but to believe in Him, and then He starts talking about heaven.

> *Let not your heart be troubled; you believe in God,*
> *believe also in Me. In My Father's house are many*
> *mansions; if it were not so, I would have told you. I*
> *go to prepare a place for you. And if I go and prepare*
> *a place for you, I will come again and receive you*
> *to Myself; that where I am, there you may be also.*
> *And where I go you know, and the way you know.*
> (John 14:1-4)

Even when His disciples had joy in seeing demons come out, Jesus redirected their focus toward another joy:

> *...rather rejoice because your names are written in*
> *heaven.*
> (Luke 10:20)

Heavenly Minded

Let's be honest, most of us don't think about heaven until someone dies or life gets very difficult. Hardships make us realize that life is as fast as a breath (Job 7:7), as temporal as grass (1 Peter 1:24), as lasting as a flower (Job 14:2), and as passing as a shadow (Ecclesiastes 6:12). It vanishes as a vapor (James 4:14). Death is as water spilled (2 Samuel 14:14), and to gain this life is to lose it (Matthew 10:39). We must put an end to the myth that "people are so heavenly minded they are no earthly good." I have yet to meet one person who is so heavenly minded that they are no earthly good. It's usually the opposite—people are so earthly minded that they are no heavenly good. God commands us to be heavenly minded (Colossians 3:2). We are not trying to escape earth by thinking about heaven, but the hope of heaven inspires our joy when we go through hell here on earth.

C.S. Lewis said:

> "If you read history, you will find that the Christians who did the most for the present world were just those who thought most of the next … It is since, Christians have largely ceased to think of the other world that they have become so ineffective in this."[30]

This World is Not Our Home

This world is not my home; I'm just here passing through. This life on earth is like a hotel; it's not our home. I travel a lot and I stay in hotels. Sometimes I stay in nice hotels and sometimes they're not so nice. When I travel, I bring only what's needed for the journey! I don't bring all my clothes, furniture, and books to the hotel because I am not staying there very long. I don't take a U-Haul with me everywhere I travel to speak. Every time I stay at a hotel, there is a check-out time that tells me when I have to leave. Life on earth is like living in a hotel; it's not our home. When I die, I want people to say, "He went home," not, "He left home." To do that, I must live with heaven in mind today.

If You've Lost a Loved One

grew up on a street where two of my neighbors were my best friends, Vitaliy and Vadim. We went to the same church, were the same age, and lived next to each other. We usually took the bus to school, but one day, a friend of the family offered to give us a ride in his car. That meant we didn't have to walk, wait for a bus, and take forty minutes to get to school; we could be at school in ten minutes. When we got in the car, it turned out that he had a flat tire, so he asked us to wait until he fixed it. We were already dressed for school with our backpacks on our backs, and we were looking for something to do to pass the time.

My friend Vadim had a swing in his driveway, so we decided to have fun on the swing while we waited. Vadim's swing was unlike anything I had ever seen. It was a heavy-duty metal swing that his father had welded together, and it was mounted into an asphalt driveway. The swing had two low-back benches and could seat four people. It was not the average swing you'd see in the park. While the swing was fun, it was not built with safety in mind. The space between the metal beam on the floor of the swing and the asphalt was only six to eight inches. It was really close to the ground.

Obviously, swinging high was not recommended, but kids rarely pay attention to safety rules. Fun was on our minds. While standing on the bench of the swing, we would pull on the supporting pole attached to the ground to make the swing go really fast. We had done this many times. This day, we were having a blast swinging back and forth and picking up speed. My friend and I stood up on the seats to give it more push while our other friend was sitting on the other bench. Soon, we had it swinging dangerously high. If we didn't hold onto the rails, we could fall. Two of us were standing, and one was sitting. I was standing, and my friend Vadim was sitting. We decided to swap, so I could sit, and he could stand. While we were changing places, the swing was moving as fast as it could. I landed on the seat and quickly grabbed the seat so I wouldn't fall off midair, but as Vadim tried grabbing the metal support beam, his hand slipped. He fell headfirst onto the concrete with the heavy swing coming down at him, full speed. The weight of the swing, plus the speed and the weight of two energetic kids, me being one of them, hit his skull right in front of our eyes. I watched with horror as the heavy weight of the metal beam of the swing smashed his head.

He died on the spot at 11:00 a.m. on April 11, 1995, three days before Easter. Vadim was only nine years old.

Seeing my best friend die right in front of my eyes in a such a horrific way was the most traumatizing experience I have ever encountered. There was no one in my life to help me process that experience. The school didn't provide counseling, and my parents were so busy processing it that they didn't even ask me how I was processing it. My nine-year-old self was thrown into an abyss of questions and mixed feelings. They raged within me. *Why did God take my best friend? That could have been me. Why was I left on this earth while he went to heaven? How do I erase the image from my mind of his head being smashed by the heavy metal beam?* Guilt, fear, doubt, and grief swept over me.

I was speechless—dumbfounded. Guilt overwhelmed me because Vadim and I were switching places on the swing. It could have been me that died that day. Why did God allow that tragic accident? That day, I lost a close friend, but his parents lost their eldest son.

Loss of life is tragic and extremely painful. Losing a loved one affects us deeply. In the Gospel of Luke, Simeon said to Mary concerning Jesus, "Yes, a sword will pierce through your own soul also" (Luke 2:35). When we lose someone, it's like a dagger going through our soul. The pain is unspeakable. It's different when people get old and die from old age, but Jesus would die at the prime age of thirty-three, and Mary would bury her son.

The Shadow of Death

Psalm 23 has been a source of comfort for many people going through the valley of loss. David started off by saying, "The Lord is my shepherd. He (is the one who) makes me lie down in green pastures. He leads me…He restores me." In the first three verses of the psalm, David referred to God as "He." But everything changes in verse four. David went from talking *about* God to talking directly *to* Him. What changed that? A valley!

Yea, though I walk through the valley of the shadow
of death, I will fear no evil; for You are with me; Your
rod and Your staff, they comfort me.

(Psalm 23:4)

Did you catch that? The Lord is my Shepherd who takes me into green pastures and beside the still waters, but He doesn't stop me from entering a valley. Sometimes we think that if God is truly our Shepherd, the leader of our life, we will avoid valleys of loss and death. But that doesn't seem to be the case. Instead of us skipping valleys because God is with us, He stays with us in the midst of them. "I will fear no evil; for You are with me," is direct communication with the Lord. Fear has no landing ground if we are aware of the Lord's presence. His presence brings peace and comfort; it defeats all fear and worry.

"Though I walk through the valley of the shadow of death." This valley is where we walk through loss and sometimes through death. David didn't say, "Though I walk through the valley of death..." He said, "...through the valley of the *shadow* of death." Death casts it's shadow in this valley. I once heard a story that made this verse come alive. A pastor lost his wife to cancer and was driving to her funeral with their young children. While riding in the car, his kids asked why God would take Mommy away from them. As a husband, he struggled with the same question; but at that moment, he needed to help his kids process their loss.

Coming upon a traffic light, a large semi-truck pulled up next to them. It cast a shadow on their vehicle, thus blocking the sun temporarily. When the light turned green, he let the semi-truck get ahead of them. Everywhere that truck went, there was a dark shadow. The father turned to his children and asked, if someone gets run over by the shadow of the semi-truck, will they be hurt? The kids replied, "No, a shadow doesn't hurt; it only blocks the sun from shining directly on a person." The father responded, "That's correct." Then he proceeded to ask another question, "If a semi-truck runs over a person, will it hurt them?" "Of course it would," the kids replied.

The pastor told his kids that the shadow of a monster truck called death passed over their mother. It was just a shadow of death. Real death passed over Jesus–He experienced the head-on collision with the truck of death. He died our death and then defeated that death by rising up from the grave.

Even though his response didn't answer why their mom died, it provided hope that physical death is just a shadow. While it temporarily blocks the sun and causes us to feel hopeless, we feel as though we can't see God or His work. But, as those whose Shepherd is Jesus, we walk *through* that valley of the shadow of death–we don't live there. We take courage that death is just a shadow. Physical death is just a change of address, but real death is separation from God. If we keep walking with the Lord and relying on the comfort of His Spirit, the sun will shine on us again.

> *You prepare a table before me in the presence of my enemies; You anoint my head with oil; my cup runs over. Surely goodness and mercy shall follow me all the days of my life; and I will dwell in the house of the Lord forever.*
>
> (Psalm 23:5-6)

After the four verses about the shadow of death come verses five and six. In the first four verses, the Lord is our Shepherd, but in verse five, He is our Host. As our Host, He prepares a table for us and anoints our head with oil. If we keep walking with Him, even through valleys of shadows, He will bring us out from under those shadows and up to His table. He will anoint our head with the oil of gladness. He will fill our cup until it is running over. If we find ourselves in the valley, we must not live there, but walk through it. We are never alone; our Shepherd is with us. He will not only lead us out of the valley but also reveal Himself as our Host and take us into a new season of grace and mercy.

Dealing with Loss

So, how does one walk through the valley of the shadow of death? David is the one who wrote the psalm about the Good Shepherd. David, a man after God's heart, was no stranger to loss. Let's look at one account of David walking through loss that holds simple but profound keys for us today.

After his affair with Bathsheba, God pronounced judgments on David, and one of them was that the child born to him would die. When that newborn child became ill, David did what every parent would do. He fasted, prayed, pleaded with God, lay on the ground, and refused to be consoled. He went until the end, really hoping there would be a different outcome than what had been prophesied. But the result was still the same—the loss of the child. When he heard the tragic news of that loss, he did something unusual.

> *So David arose from the ground, washed and anointed himself, and changed his clothes; and he went into the house of the LORD and worshiped. Then he went to*

*his own house; and when he requested, they set food
before him, and he ate.*

(2 Samuel 12:20)

David, the great king and psalmist of Israel, walked through the valley of the shadow of death.

He arose from the ground, as the Scriptures tell us, after *"having done all, to stand"* (Ephesians 6:13). We have to stand in what we know, not lay in what we feel. We have to stand after we have done all that we know to do. The outcome is in God's hands.

He washed himself. We have to use the water of the Word to cleanse our soul. Disappointment is like dirt. It can stick to our souls and make us doubt God in the future. "You are already clean because of the word which I have spoken to you" (John 15:3). "That He might sanctify and cleanse her with the washing of water by the word" (Ephesians 5:26).

He anointed himself. After washing himself, he put on oil. As Christians, during moments of loss, we rely on the comfort of the Holy Spirit. We can build ourselves up by praying in the Holy Spirit. "But you, beloved, building yourselves up on your most holy faith, praying in the Holy Spirit" (Jude 20). The presence of the Holy Spirit will bring healing to the heart that's broken.

He changed his clothes. Clothing represents our mental attitude. We can fall into a victim mentality—*Poor little me; why do bad things happen to me all the time?* These thoughts can take root in our heart during times of loss. When facing an evil day, we should dress up in the armor of God that we might be able to stand against the schemes of the devil. "Therefore take up the whole armor of God, that you may be able to withstand in the evil day, and having done all, to stand" (Ephesians 6:13).

God's attitude helps us to withstand in the evil day so we can stand. The chapter on the armor of God doesn't tell us how to fight but how to stay firm. The key to standing in the hard days is our spiritual armor.

He went to the house of the Lord. David could have allowed his loss to drive him from the house of God, but instead, he chose to go to God's house. We should develop a habit of going to church when times are good and even more, when times are hard.

Please note that when Peter and John were threatened by religious leaders for healing the lame man, they went to their own friends. "And being let go, they went to their own companions and reported all that the chief priests and elders had said to them" (Acts 4:23). The apostles relied on their brothers and sisters in difficult times. While some may see loss as an excuse to run from God's house, we should go to church even more when faced with tragedy.

He worshipped. Another man of God, Job, did the same thing when he lost his family. "Then Job arose, tore his robe, and shaved his head; and he fell to the ground and worshiped" (Job 1:20). Part of the grieving for both David and Job was to worship God. We might wonder, *How could someone worship in the midst of such a difficult time?* Please remember that we will either surrender or slander God in seasons of loss. If we don't worship, we will become bitter and our heart will harden toward the Lord.

He ate. David fasted for seven days when the child was sick, but then he sat down to eat. Sometimes when we experience loss, we lose our appetite for the Word of God. It feels dull and boring to read it. A lack of desire to do anything, including reading God's Word, is normal, but staying in that state is dangerous.

We must force-feed ourselves with God's Word. Appetites grow with eating. "But He answered and said, 'It is written, Man shall not live by bread alone, but by every word that proceeds from the mouth of God'" (Matthew 4:4). We live by the words that proceed from God's mouth. God speaks when we read the Bible. God's Word is spiritual nourishment for a weary soul and healing for a broken heart. In times of loss, it may be tempting to read the Bible to find answers, but most likely, God will use His Word to bring strength to our souls, rather than answers.

He comforted Bathsheba. God brings His comfort to us so He can bring it through us to others. God's comfort must be shared. We are to be channels of that comfort, not bottles of it. "[W]ho comforts us in all our tribulation, that we may be able to comfort those who are in any trouble, with the comfort with which we ourselves are comforted by God" (2 Corinthians 1:4). God comforts us so we can comfort others. That's what David did. The comfort he received from God's presence, he shared with Bathsheba.

By Faith We Understand

It's important, during times of loss, to trust in God, even when we can't see Him. When we can't seem to understand what is happening, our trust must be in God. God invites us to trust in Him, not in our own understanding. "Trust in the LORD with all your heart, and lean not on your own understanding" (Proverbs 3:5). To trust in your own understanding is to lean on your own ability to make sense of everything. That's very dangerous.

Our understanding can either be enlightened by the Lord or darkened by the enemy (Ephesians 1:18; 4:18). When we trust God, even when we don't fully understand, we will find peace that surpasses all understanding (Philippians 4:7). God's ways are higher than our ways; His ways are beyond us finding them out (Romans 11:33; Isaiah 55:9).

At first, it may seem like blind faith, but faith is not blind if it sees God. Our understanding is what might be blind because it can be darkened by the enemy. While the Bible tells us to love the Lord with all our understanding (Matthew 22:37 LSV), we must not elevate our understanding to the place of a god. Our mind, our reason, and our ability to understand must bow to God's Word, not the other way around.

Trusting in God doesn't mean we turn off our brain. Our mind matters, but it's not our master; it's our servant. God is our master. We accept a lot of things from God by faith, not by understanding or reasoning. I still don't understand how a brown cow can eat green grass and produce white milk. But I drink milk, regardless of my lack of understanding. Our faith in God enlightens our understanding. Instead of our mind educating our faith, it's our faith that should educate our mind.

> *By faith we understand that the worlds were framed*
> *by the word of God, so that the things which are seen*
> *were not made of things which are visible.*
>
> (Hebrews 11:3)

Lord, Teach Us How to Pray

Prayer is huge for Christians, but many believers don't know what to do in prayer. Are you wondering how to pray or what to pray for? You are not alone! The disciples asked Jesus the same question.

What is prayer?

Let's define prayer first. Prayer is a cry, a conversation, and a confrontation. According to Matthew 7:7, prayer has to have three parts: asking, seeking, and knocking. Asking deals with presenting our petitions—it's when we ask for what we need. Seeking deals with devotion—it's when we seek God's presence. Knocking deals with intercession—it's when we pray for others. Prayer is like a triangle made up of three corners. I find many people don't make room for all these angles in prayer and, therefore, their prayers are not very effective. Our prayers should be spontaneous and strategic at the same time.

Who do we pray to?

We don't pray to Mary or to saints; we pray to God. When talking about prayer, Jesus focused more on the one to whom we direct our prayer, than on how prayer should be done. He taught the disciples to pray "Our Father." He told us that prayer is about the Father, not a formula. We are God's children; He is our Father. We are Jesus' bride; He is our Bridegroom. We are God's friends; He is our Friend. This conversation with Him should be natural.

There is something I want to address, though. Sound biblical theology teaches us to pray to the Father God through the name of the Lord Jesus Christ and by the power and quickening of the Holy Spirit! Jesus, too, tells us to pray to the Father through His name.

> ...whatever you ask the Father in My name He may give you.
>
> (John 15:16)

> And whatever you ask in My name, that I will do, that the Father may be glorified in the Son. If you ask anything in My name, I will do it.
>
> (John 14:13-14)

The Holy Spirit comes into the picture as well.

> Likewise the Spirit also helps in our weaknesses. For we do not know what we should pray for as we ought,

but the Spirit Himself makes intercession for us with groanings which cannot be uttered.

(Romans 8:26)

The Holy Spirit is your prayer partner.

Should you pray out loud?

John Bunyan said, "When you pray, rather let your hearts be without words than your words without a heart." While I love this quote and appreciate the heart behind it, I want to say that prayer is more than a thought; it is a communication of that thought. The Bible does mention silent prayers. Abraham's servant spoke to God in his heart (Genesis 24:45). Hannah spoke to God in her heart (1 Samuel 1:10-15). God, who sees the heart, can hear the thoughts.

However, there is also clear biblical instruction to make our prayers vocal. This doesn't mean we have to yell or grab a microphone. Psalm 4:3 says, "...the LORD will hear when I call to Him." Calling is vocal.

In another place, "O LORD, God of my salvation, I have cried out day and night before You. Let my prayer come before You; incline Your ear to my cry" (Psalm 88:1-2). Crying is usually not in your heart, it's verbal. "Evening and morning and at noon I will pray, and cry aloud, and He shall hear my voice" (Psalm 55:17). This is not just crying out but crying aloud. In Isaiah 24:14, it talks about people lifting their voices and crying aloud: "They shall lift up their voice, they shall sing; For the majesty of the Lord. They shall cry aloud from the sea."

There are more examples of this in the Bible:

- In their bondage, the children of Israel cried to the Lord (Exodus 2:23-24).

- Moses cried out to the Lord for miraculous assistance (Exodus 15:25).

- Samuel cried out to the Lord (1 Samuel 7:8-9).

- David cried out to Lord (Psalm 138:3).

- Jonah cried out to the Lord (Jonah 2:1-2).

- Bartimaeus cried out to Jesus for healing of blindness (Mark 10:46-62). In fact, when people told Bartimaeus to shut up, he cried out even louder. Loud prayers don't annoy Jesus, but they might irritate some of His followers.

Jesus used His voice in His prayers to the Father. It says in John 17:1 that He "lifted up His eyes and said." As well as in Luke 23:46 that Jesus "cried out with a loud voice."

The Apostles "raised their voice to God with one accord" (Acts 4:24), In another instance, Stephen "knelt down and cried out with a loud voice" (Acts 7:59-60).

I want to encourage you to practice both silent prayer and loud prayer. Your mouth speaks out of the abundance of the heart. So let your mouth speak. Also, Jesus instructed us to "say" our prayers:

> *So He said to them, "When you pray, say..."*
>
> (Luke 11:2)

The Lord didn't just tell us to think our prayers but to say them. There are many promises as well to those who cry out to God in prayer:

The eyes of the LORD are on the righteous, and His ears are open to their cry.

(Psalm 34:15)

Call to Me, and I will answer you, and show you great and mighty things, which you do not know.

(Jeremiah 33:3)

Should you pray in the morning or evening?

The short answer is to pray always, without ceasing. While we should live in constant communion with the Lord, we should also prioritize prayer times. It's the difference between "devotion" and "devotions." Devotion is your life given to Jesus, but devotions is your time spent with Him. Some like to call it quiet time or time of prayer. I am more of a morning prayer person; I always have been. I see a lot of evidence for morning prayer in the Bible, but the Bible also mentions praying at night.

Here are some of my reasons for praying in the morning:

- Abraham rose early in the morning to offer Isaac (Genesis 22:3).

- Moses rose early in the morning to build an altar (Exodus 24:4).

- David said that God would hear his voice in the morning (Psalm 5:3).

- God gave manna to Israel in the morning (Exodus 16:12).

- God commanded priests to put fire on the altar every morning (Leviticus 6:12).

- Jesus prayed in the morning (Mark 1:35).

Morning prayer is about putting God first in your day. It builds discipline in your life. I like what John Bunyan said about morning prayer:

> "He who runs from God in the morning will hardly find Him at the close of the day; nor will he who begins with the world and the vanities thereof, in the first place, be very capable of walking with God all the day after. It is he who finds God in his closet that will carry the savor of him into his house, his shop, and his more open conversation."

E.M. Bounds is the prayer apostle; his books on prayer have impacted many men and women of God. This is what he said about morning prayer:

> "The men who have done the most for God in this world have been early on their knees. He who fritters away the early morning, its opportunity and freshness, in other pursuits than seeking God will make poor headway seeking him the rest of the day. If God is not first in our thoughts and efforts in the morning, he will be in the last place the remainder of the day."

If you want to build a consistent prayer life, start early in the morning and prepare yourself for it by going to sleep earlier. God doesn't want you to pray like a zombie, being sleep-deprived.

When it comes to evening prayers, Jesus prayed all night, but not all the time. After that all night prayer, He chose His disciples (Luke 6:12-13). One time, after a full day of ministry, Jesus went to pray at night. I can only image how tiring that was for His physical body. But after that prayer, He walked on water to His disciples (Matthew 14:23-25). I am not saying that if you pray all night, you will walk on water, but you will surely see a shift in your life.

Jacob wrestled with God at night and never walked the same after that (Genesis 32:22-31). I will be honest; I don't practice night prayers or all-night prayers regularly. Occasionally, I do, because they bring a different level of breakthrough. All-night prayer is more like a workout where you start to feel the burn. You can run out of things to pray after an hour or two and the body starts getting weary, but if you continue and press in, a wave of God's glory comes in, clarity comes, and a deeper connection to the Lord is made. Try it sometime!

The following verses give us insight about night and day prayer:

> *That Your eyes may be open toward this temple day and night, toward the place where You said You would put Your name, that You may hear the prayer which Your servant makes toward this place.*
>
> (2 Chronicles 6:20)

> *I have set watchmen on your walls, O Jerusalem; They shall never hold their peace day or night. You who make mention of the LORD, do not keep silent, and give Him no rest till He establishes and till He makes Jerusalem a praise in the earth.*
>
> (Isaiah 62:6)

O Lord, the God of my salvation, I have cried out by day and in the night before You.

(Psalm 88:1)

And then as a widow to the age of eighty-four. She never left the temple, serving night and day with fastings and prayers.

(Luke 2:37)

As we night and day keep praying most earnestly that we may see your face, and may complete what is lacking in your faith?

(1 Thessalonians 3:10)

Now she who is a widow indeed and who has been left alone, has fixed her hope on God and continues in entreaties and prayers night and day.

(1 Timothy 5:5)

I thank God, whom I serve with a clear conscience the way my forefathers did, as I constantly remember you in my prayers night and day.

(2 Timothy 1:3)

What should be my physical posture in prayer?

The most common prayer posture is kneeling. Daniel kneeled in prayer (Daniel 6:10). Stephen prayed kneeling (Acts 7:60). Peter prayed kneeling (Acts 9:40). Paul prayed kneeling (Acts 20:36; 21:5; Ephesians 3:14-16).

When it comes to prayer, the posture of the heart is the most important. But we see David sitting in prayer (2 Samuel 7:18). Jesus talked about standing in prayer (Mark 11:25). Another posture is facing the ground, Jesus prayed like that in the garden of Gethsemane (Matthew 26:39).

We can lift our hands in prayer (1 Timothy 2:8). As well as lift our eyes to heaven as Jesus did when He prayed (John 17:1). Elijah prayed placing his face between his knees (1 Kings 18:42). That might not be comfortable or possible for some. One tax collector pounded his chest during prayer, but that was more out of deep sorrow and repentance (Luke 18:13). It's probably not a formula for us to imitate.

Where should I pray?

We can pray anywhere! Men of God in the Old Testament had altars where they prayed to God. Noah, Abraham, Jacob, Moses, Joshua, Gideon, Samuel, David, Solomon and even Elijah prayed at the altar. Later on in the Bible, people prayed in temples! This is why we refer to our prayer place as an altar. This doesn't mean that we have to build an actual altar in our prayer room.

Jesus is our model. He prayed in the wilderness (Luke 5:16), on a mountain (Luke 6:12-13), in a garden (Matthew 26:36-56), or another solitary place (Mark 1:35). Jesus told us to go into our room to pray (Matthew 6:6). Any place we choose where we want to talk to God, is that altar.

I want you to notice that Jesus said to go into a room to pray. He didn't say just open your eyes on your bed under warm blankets and talk to God. Though God can hear any prayer, something happens when you get out of your bed, find a quiet place, and spend time with Him without distractions.

As Christians, we are also told to gather with others to pray. That's why God's house is called a house of prayer (Matthew 21:13). Early believers waiting for the coming of the Holy Spirit gathered together to pray (Acts 1:14). Some people don't like corporate prayer and pray only in private. The Bible instructs us to do both. Here are some verses that show us the power of praying with others:

> *Again I say to you that if two of you agree on earth concerning anything that they ask, it will be done for them by My Father in heaven.*
>
> (Matthew 18:19)

> *These all continued with one accord in prayer and supplication, with the women and Mary the mother of Jesus, and with His brothers.*
>
> (Acts 1:14)

> *So when they heard that, they raised their voice to God with one accord and said: "Lord, You are God, who made heaven and earth and the sea, and all that is in them."*
>
> (Acts 4:24)

What should I say in prayer?

This is probably the most asked question! Often people aren't sure what to pray about. My seminary instructor gave us the "TACOS" prayer.

> T for thanksgiving.
> A for adoration.
> C for confession.
> O for others.
> S for self.

These are some good guidelines that you can use for your prayer time. This doesn't mean that you have to make it rigid, going through each one of the points. It's okay to be spontaneous and systematic at the same time.

Thanking God for what He did for you.

Pray without ceasing, in everything give thanks; for this is the will of God in Christ Jesus for you.
                                    (1 Thessalonians 5:17-18)

Praise God for who He is.

Therefore by Him let us continually offer the sacrifice of praise to God, that is, the fruit of our lips, giving thanks to His name.
                                    (Hebrews 13:15)

Confess your sins.

If we confess our sins, He is faithful and just to forgive us our sins and to cleanse us from all unrighteousness.
(1 John 1:9)

Ask God for what you need.

Ask, and it will be given to you; seek, and you will find; knock, and it will be opened to you.
(Matthew 7:7-11)

Intercede for others.

Therefore I exhort first of all that supplications, prayers, intercessions, and giving of thanks be made for all men.
(1 Timothy 2:1)

Pray in tongues.

For if I pray in a tongue, my spirit prays, but my understanding is unfruitful.
(1 Corinthians 14:14)

Wait on the Lord.

But those who wait on the LORD shall renew their strength; they shall mount up with wings like eagles, they shall run and not be weary, they shall walk and not faint.

(Isaiah 40:31)

Wait on the LORD; be of good courage, and He shall strengthen your heart; wait, I say, on the LORD!

(Psalm 27:14)

Listen to God.

My sheep hear My voice, and I know them, and they follow Me.

(John 10:27)

Some other Biblical models of prayer are The Tabernacle Prayer, The Lord's Prayer, Spiritual Warfare Prayer, The Prayer of Jabez, and The Names of God. Here are their basic breakdowns:

The Tabernacle Prayer

(The Tabernacle of Moses serves as a model for prayer–you can find its structure in Exodus 25, 27, 30.)

1. Brazen Altar - Thank God for the Cross.

2. Laver - Ask Jesus to sanctify you.

3. Menorah - Ask the Lord to know the Holy Spirit.

4. Showbread - Read God's Word.

5. Altar of Incense - Worship the Lord.

6. Mercy Seat - Intercede for others.

The Lord's Prayer

(Praying through Matthew 6:9-13.)

1. Our Father - Proclaim who He is and who you are.

2. Hallowed be Your Name - Worship His name.

3. Your Kingdom Come - Pray for His agenda.

4. Give us this Day Our Daily Bread - Ask for personal requests.

5. Forgive us Our Debts - Forgive others in prayer.

6. Don't Lead us into Temptation - Present your weaknesses to God.

7. Deliver us from Evil - Put on the armor of God.

8. Yours is the Power - Express faith in God's ability.

Spiritual Warfare Prayer

(This prayer goes through God's armor, based on Ephesians 6:11-18.)

1. The Belt - I believe Your truth; help me to live by the truth.

2. The Breastplate - Thank You for righteousness; help me to live righteously.

3. The Shoes - Thank You for peace; help me to be an ambassador of Your peace.

4. The Shield - I trust in Your Word; my heart is protected; I resist every evil thought.

5. The Helmet - I thank You for salvation; I reject every lie attacking my mind.

6. The Sword - I will hide Your Word in my heart and use it as a sword to defeat the works of darkness.

The Prayer of Jabez

(Goes through the prayer of Jabez in 1 Chronicles 4:9-10.)

1. "Oh that You would bless me" - Praying for blessing.

2. "Enlarge my territory" - Asking for influence.

3. "Your hand be upon me" - Seeking God's presence.

4. "Keep me from evil" - Asking God for protection.

5. "That I may not cause pain" - Asking God to make us a blessing.

The Names of God

(Elaborates on the power of His name; Proverbs 18:10.)

Jehovah Jireh (Genesis 22:13-14) – The Lord my Provider.

Jehovah Rapha (Exodus 16:26) – The Lord my Healer.

Jehovah Nissi (Exodus 17:15) – The Lord my Banner.

Jehovah M'Kaddesh (Exodus 31:13) – The Lord my Sanctifier.

Jehovah Shalom (Judges 6:24) – The Lord my Peace.

Jehovah Rohi (Psalm 23:1) – The Lord my Shepherd.

Jehovah Sabbaoth (Isaiah 6:3) – The Lord of Hosts or Armies (My Defense).

Jehovah Tsidkenu (Jeremiah 23:6) – The Lord my Righteousness.

Jehovah Shammah (Ezekiah 48:35) – The Lord Who is Ever Present.

APPENDIX 4

How to Fast

O ur human body was designed by God to be able to fast. Did you know that when you sleep, you are fasting? That's why the first meal of the day is called *break*fast—it's when you break your fast. Scientific research tells us that a lot of repairing takes place in our bodies when we fast. So, good news—you've already been sort of secretly fasting all your life!

What is Fasting?

Biblical fasting is not starvation or an involuntary absence of food; it is abstaining from food for spiritual reasons. Fasting is not a hunger strike, and it is not a diet—a diet focuses on helping you lose weight. Fasting is a spiritual discipline that draws you closer to God. It helps you to find fulfillment in God's calling on your life, as well as subdue your flesh with all its conflicts. You can fast for different reasons, such as to overcome problems and challenges, or to restore your hunger and passion for God.

Types of Fasts

There are different types of fasts. There is an **absolute fast**, going without food or water, sometimes referred to as a **dry fast**. Moses did two forty-day absolute fasts virtually back-to-back (Exodus 34:28; Deuteronomy 9:9, 18). The city of Nineveh fasted like this for three days (Jonah 3:7) as well as the apostle Paul after his encounter with the Lord (Acts 9:9). Caution: This should NOT be undertaken for more than three days, and it should only be done if you have a clear directive from the Lord and are in good health.

Another fast is called a **normal fast** or a **full fast**. This is when you don't eat and you only drink water. We believe that Jesus went on this type of fast for forty days. The Bible says He ate nothing, but it doesn't mention that He didn't drink anything: "…being tempted for forty days by the devil. And in those days He ate nothing, and afterward, when they had ended, He was hungry" (Luke 4:2). Usually, if a person in the Bible didn't drink anything during their fast, Scripture would point that out.

A **partial fast**, commonly referred to as a **Daniel fast**, is where you abstain from certain foods. This fast usually includes eating no meat, no sweets, no dairy or other pleasant foods–only soups, fruits, and vegetables. This fast is named after the prophet Daniel: "I ate no pleasant food, no meat or wine came into my mouth, nor did I anoint myself at all, till three whole weeks were fulfilled" (Daniel 10:3). For me, this is the hardest fast. I don't think I have ever done more than seven days because I don't like fasting and thinking about food at the same time. Plus, eating an entire meal and still feeling hungry is a tougher challenge for me than simply not eating at all.

The last type of fast is a **corporate fast**. Your private fasting should be done in secret as Jesus instructed in Matthew 6:16, but there is also a public fast which is proclaimed by leaders. There are a few biblical examples of this, such as:

- The prophet Samuel calling an entire nation to a fast (1 Samuel 7:6).

- Esther calling the Jewish people to a fast (Esther 4:16).

- Ezra proclaiming a fast (Ezra 8:21-23).

- The pagan king of Nineveh declaring a fast for his nation (Jonah 3:5).

- The disciples fasting and ministering to the Lord (Acts 13:2-3).

As a reminder, we are to examine our hearts so that we practice periods of fasting to be noticed by the Lord, not by the eyes of man.

How to Fast

Set a goal. No matter what type of fast you begin, you must have a reason and a goal! Be specific. Why are you fasting? Do you want to get closer to God and be more sensitive to the spiritual realm? Do you need direction in life's decisions, healing, restoration of your marriage, help with family issues, or wisdom? Are you facing financial difficulties? Ask the Holy Spirit for guidance. Decide what to fast for and present it constantly to God in prayer.

Decide on the type of fast. The type of fast you choose is between you and the Lord. You could go on a full fast, where you only drink liquids. You may desire to fast like Daniel, who abstained from sweets and meats, and the only liquid he drank was water. Pay attention to what the Holy Spirit leads you to do and do it.

Choose length. Also, decide how long you will fast. Remember that you may fast as long as you like, as the Lord leads. Be courteous enough to inform those who prepare meals for you or share meals with you about your plans to fast. Most people can easily fast from one to three days, but you may feel God's grace to go longer, even 21 to 40 days. Use wisdom and pray for guidance. Beginners are advised to start slowly.

Plan ahead. Choose days that fit your schedule, take into consideration that you might feel extra tired. When you fast, your body eliminates toxins from your system. This can cause mild discomfort, such as headaches and irritability during withdrawal from caffeine and sugars. And naturally, you will have hunger pains. Hunger is a common side effect of any fast. Avoiding water can make you feel even hungrier, since water helps increase satiety. If you don't eat food or drink water, your body begins to crave fuel. You will likely feel fatigued, dizzy, and weak. David said of his fasting, "My knees are weak through fasting, and my flesh is feeble from lack of fatness" (Psalm 109:24). One of the other things we often feel during a fast is irritability. As the hunger builds up, you're bound to feel cranky. Mood swings are pretty common. Also, when you're tired and hungry, it can be difficult to concentrate at school or work. So, limit your activity, use good common sense, and exercise moderately. Take time to rest.

Set aside time each day to quiet yourself before the Lord, meditate on His Word, and write down what He might be saying to you. Fasting brings about miraculous results. You are following Jesus' example when you fast. Spend time listening to praise and worship music. Constantly read and meditate on the Word. Let the hunger pangs remind you to stop everything and pray–and pray as often as you can throughout the day. Get away from normal distractions as much as possible, and keep your heart and mind set on seeking the face of God.

Make a decision to end the fast slowly. Of course, how much time you need to resume your regular diet depends on what you fast from and for how long. If it was only a one-day fast, then usually there is no harm in resuming normal eating. If you go for more than three days, you must begin eating solid food very gradually; eat small portions or snacks. When the time comes to end your fast, eating solid foods too soon and/or overeating can be extremely dangerous to your digestive system.

Thank You for Reading

We hope this book was a blessing to you. To help you dive deeper, we also offer a study guide and e-course videos to accompany it. These resources are great for weekly small-group discussions!

We also offer reading plans on the YouVersion Bible App to enhance your study and integrate God's Word into your daily life.

If this book was a blessing to you, would you also consider leaving a review on Amazon or Goodreads and sharing it on your social media? This will go a long way in helping others discover this book and grow in their walk with God.

For more information and access to all our resources, please visit www.pastorvlad.org.

Partner with Us

Vladimir Savchuk Ministries offers a number of biblical resources such as courses, videos, reading plans, and books that have been translated into more than a dozen languages, all free of charge. We are also involved in humanitarian aid around the world, helping those in need.

Our desire is that people from every nation would be able to learn about Jesus Christ and grow in their walk with God. Would you consider offering a one-time gift or becoming a partner to help us continue providing these free resources to people around the globe?

We believe that everyone should have access to free biblical content, and your donations and support help make it possible.

To learn more about our ministry's vision and impact, or to donate, please visit www.pastorvlad.org/donate.

Other Books

 Break Free
How to Get Free and Stay Free

 Single, Ready to Mingle
*God's Principles for Relating,
Dating, and Mating*

 Fight Back
Moving from Deliverance to Dominion

Fast Forward

Accelerate Your Spiritual Life Through Fasting

Host the Holy Ghost

Available everywhere books are sold in paperback, electronic, audio version. You can also download a free PDF on www.pastorvlad.org/books

Stay Connected

facebook.com/vladhungrygen

twitter.com/vladhungrygen

instagram.com/vladhungrygen

youtube.com/vladimirsavchuk

www.pastorvlad.org

www.vladschool.com

If you have a testimony from reading this book, let us know www.pastorvlad.org/testimony

If you wish to post about this e-book on your social media, please use tag @vladhungrygen and use #pastorvlad hashtag.

Endnotes

CHAPTER 2

1 Vladimir Savchuk, *Break Free* (2018), 151.

2 C.S. Lewis, *The Problem of Pain* (1940; repr., San Francisco: Harper San Francisco, 2001), 91.

CHAPTER 3

3 Viktor E. Frankl, *Man's Search for Meaning, Gift Edition* (Beacon Press, 2015), 5.

CHAPTER 5

4 James Strong, *A Concise Dictionary of the Words in the Greek Testament and The Hebrew Bible* (Bellingham, WA: Logos Bible Software, 2009), s.v. "3875-76. טוֹל (lote)."

5 Ibid., s.v. "4413. πρῶτος (prótos)."

6 John Bunyan, *A Holy Life; or, The Beauty of Christianity*, vol. 2, 537.

7 Strong, *A Concise Dictionary of the Words in the Greek Testament and The Hebrew Bible*, s.v. "1577. ἐκκλησία (ekklésia)."

CHAPTER 6

8 Savchuk, *Break Free*, 99-100.

CHAPTER 7

9   *Yonggi Cho's Testimony.* Reach Our Nation. 10 May 2009, https:// reachournation.blogspot.com/2009/05/yonggi-chos-testimony.html.

10 *David Yonggi Cho and Yoido Full Gospel Church.* Flower Pentecostal Heritage Center. 8 September 2022, https://ifphc. wordpress.com/2022/09/08/david-yonggi-cho-and-yoido-ful l-gospel-church-the-story-behind-the-worlds-largest-church/.

11 *David Yonggi Cho.* Wikipedia. https://en.wikipedia.org/wiki/ David_Yonggi_Cho.

12 Laura Wamsley, "Judge Orders Boy Who Started Oregon Wildfire To Pay $36 Million In Restitution," *NPR*, 22 May 2018, https:// www.npr.org/sections/thetwo-way/2018/05/22/613374984/ judge-orders-boy-who-started-oregon-wildfire-to-pay-36-million-in-re stitution.

13 Matt Rascon and R. Stickney, "Cocos Fire Arsonist Learns Fate at Sentencing Hearing," *NBC 7 San Diego*, 28 May 2015, www. nbcsandiego.com/news/local/cocos-fire-arsonist-to-learn-fat e-at-sentencing-hearing/53811/.

14 Michael Parrish, "10-Year-Old with Matches Started a California Wildfire," *The New York Times*, 1 November 2007, www.nytimes. com/2007/11/01/us/01wildfire.html.

CHAPTER 9

15 Dave Roberson, *The Walk of the Spirit the Walk of Power: The Vital Role of Praying in Tongues* (Dave Roberson Ministries, 1999).

16 Strong, *A Concise Dictionary of the Words in the Greek Testament and The Hebrew Bible,* "2786. Κηφᾶς (Képhas)."

17 *Our Daily Bread*, December 29, 1993.

CHAPTER 10

18 Edward Group, DC, "The Stages of Fasting: What Happens to Your Body When You Fast?" *Dr. Group's Healthy Living Articles*, 24 Oct. 2021, explore.globalhealing.com/ stages-of-fasting-what-happens-when-you-fast/.

19 R. Michael Anson et al., "Intermittent Fasting Dissociates Beneficial Effects of Dietary Restriction on Glucose Metabolism and Neuronal Resistance to Injury from Calorie Intake," *Proceedings of the National Academy of Sciences* 100, no. 10 (2003): 6216–6220, https://doi. org/10.1073/pnas.1035720100.

20 "How Fasting Can Benefit Your Mental Health," ed. Dan
    Brennan, MD, *WebMD*, 25 Oct. 2021, www.webmd.com/diet/
    psychological-benefits-of-fasting.

21 Edward Group, DC, "The Stages of Fasting: What Happens
    to Your Body When You Fast?" *Dr. Group's Healthy Living
    Articles*, 24 Oct. 2021, https://explore.globalhealing.com/
    stages-of-fasting-what-happens-when-you-fast/.

22 "Can You Fast If You Have Diabetes?" ed. Michael Dansinger,
    WebMD, 12 Dec. 2022, www.webmd.com/diabetes/fasting-diabetes.

23 Matt Berger, "How Intermittent Fasting Can Help
    Lower Inflammation," ed. David Mills, *Healthline*,
    22 Aug. 2019, www.healthline.com/health-news/
    fasting-can-help-ease-inflammation-in-the-body.

24 Tinsley GM, La Bounty PM, "Effects of Intermittent Fasting on Body
    Composition and Clinical Health Markers in Humans," *Nutrition
    Reviews*, Oxford University Press, 2015, pubmed.ncbi.nlm.nih.
    gov/26374764/.

25 C. L. Goodrick et al., "Effects of Intermittent Feeding upon Growth
    and Life Span in Rats," *Gerontology*, U.S. National Library of
    Medicine, 1982, pubmed.ncbi.nlm.nih.gov/7117847/.

CHAPTER 11

26 Strong, *A Concise Dictionary of the Words in the Greek Testament and
    The Hebrew Bible*, s.v. "2076. חָבַז (zabach)."

27 C. S. Lewis, *Mere Christianity* (C.S. Lewis Signature Classics) (New
    York: HarperCollins, Kindle Edition), 86.

CHAPTER 13

28 Elisabeth Elliot, *Through the Gates of Splendor* (Tyndale
    Momentum, 1981).

29 Samuel Chand, *Leadership Pain: The Classroom for Growth* (Thomas
    Nelson, 2015).

APPENDIX 1

30 Lewis, *Mere Christianity*, 134.